EIGHT SCHOOLS
CAMPUS AND CULTURE

EIGHT SCHOOLS
CAMPUS AND CULTURE

Robert Spencer Barnett

PAWSON PARK PRESS

BRANFORD
CONNECTICUT

This Book is Dedicated to the Memory of My Son Spencer and My Brother John

The Lawrenceville School
Upper House

PAWSON PARK PRESS
211 PAWSON ROAD
BRANFORD CONNECTICUT

©Robert Spencer Barnett 2018

CONTENTS

PREFACE 6

1 EDUCATION OF YOUTH IN AMERICA 12
Purpose and pedagogy

2 THE WHOLE STUDENT: TEACHING AND LEARNING 26
Colleges and college preparatory schools

3 THE WHOLE STUDENT: BOARDING AND BONDING 42
Origins of the family boarding academy

4 THE WHOLE STUDENT: DIVERSITY AND INCLUSION 56
Disruption of the WASP culture

5 THE WHOLE STUDENT: BODY AND SOUL 68
The sacred and the profane

6 THE WHOLE CAMPUS: NATURAL SETTING AND TOWN 80
From Henry David Thoreau to Rachael Carson

7 THE WHOLE CAMPUS: PHYSICAL AND FINANCIAL PLANNING 92
Not everything planned is built, and not everything built is planned

8 THE WHOLE CAMPUS: ART AND ARCHITECTURE 106
Durability, convenience and beauty

9 THE WHOLE STUDENT AND THE WHOLE CAMPUS 124
The design of a campus and the culture of a school

APPENDIX CAMPUS MAPS AND COMPARATIVE DATA 135

BIBLIOGRAPHY, ACKNOWLEDGMENTS, PHOTO CREDITS 147

Kent School
Aerial View

Preface:

THE COURSE OF MY CAREER has been shaped by campuses. Most of my life, I've been either a student living on a campus, an architect working on campus buildings, a planner managing campus building projects, or an author writing about campus planning and architecture. My goal in researching and writing this book is to better understand how the design of a particular campus reveals the culture of the school.

The campuses that I've chosen to study belong to members of the Eight Schools Association (ESA): Choate Rosemary Hall, Deerfield Academy, The Hotchkiss School, The Lawrenceville School, Northfield Mount Hermon School, Phillips Academy Andover, Phillips Exeter Academy, and St. Paul's School. They are independent college preparatory boarding schools (prep schools) located in New England and New Jersey. While limiting the scope to this group may seem overly restrictive—dare I say, exclusive—I believe that these schools embody most of the opportunities and challenges that exist at peer institutions throughout the northeastern United States.

I've explored campus culture in four broad themes that, together, shape the whole student: teaching and learning; boarding and bonding; diversity and inclusion; and body and soul[1] (chapters two through five). These themes interact with the natural and built environment that shape the whole campus: the natural setting and town; physical and financial planning; and art and architecture (chapters six through eight). These chapters are bracketed by Chapter One—an overview of public and private secondary education in the United States from colonial times to the present—and Chapter Nine—which connects the whole student with the whole campus. An appendix presents comparative data of the eight schools in the form of fast facts and annotated maps.

I've read secondary sources, including many thoughtful campus-specific and educationally general studies. My primary research, however, consists of multiple campus visits that afforded an opportunity to photograph buildings and landscapes, search the archives, and meet with buildings and grounds directors. This methodology, though hardly original, produces an awareness that can only be gained by direct experience.

Embedded in the following account of my experience as a student at Kent School in the 1960s, are themes that I explore in subsequent chapters.

SIMPLICITY OF LIFE, DIRECTNESS OF PURPOSE, SELF-RELIANCE

I am a member, to use Thomas Jefferson's phrase, of the "natural aristocracy." Jefferson's aspiration for American education was that "given a chance—equal opportunity—children from undistinguished backgrounds might compete successfully against those of the 'artificial aristocracy.'"[2] Many parents of school-age children believe prep schools are for the privileged, the "artificial aristocracy." I grew up, however, in a predominantly working class town in the Hudson Valley, one with roots in colonial times, and populated in the late nineteenth-and

Kent School
The Merry Pranksters 1963

early-twentieth-centuries by European immigrants and displaced African - Americans. No one I knew went to prep school, nor had my parents or ancestors.[3]

In the fall of 1959, I started my third form year (ninth grade) at Kent, then an all-boys boarding school in northwestern Connecticut. There are many reasons parents send their children to boarding school. In my case, the local high school was academically marginal, and my parents were struggling with elder care at home. While the public school offered several "tracks," one leading to college, Kent has always been solely a college preparatory school. My coursework included four years of English, mathematics, French, and theology; three years of history; two years of Latin; one chemistry course; and several art appreciation courses. One of the first courses taken by incoming students was "how to study." Class size was small, the faculty attentive, and the coursework rigorous. The result: more than half of my male classmates were accepted at Ivy League universities.

Kent's motto—articulated by the school's founder and first headmaster Father Frederick H. Sill (1906–1939[4])–is *Temperantia, Fiducia, Constantina:* Simplicity of Life, Directness of Purpose, Self-reliance.[5] We were expected to develop good character as well as achieve good grades. Character was inducted by religion, discipline, and manual labor. We attended evening prayer daily and Holy Eucharist on Sunday. Theology was an integral part of the curriculum.

We ate our meals together at long tables presided over by sixth formers (seniors). The food—carried to the table by underformers—started at the head and by the time it reached me and my fellow "rabble," there was little left. The rabble were allowed to go around to other tables to "scrounge" for left-overs. I figured the best way to avoid starvation and the indignity of scrounging was to volunteer for dish crew. Every boy had a job and boys on dish crew ate well in the kitchen. Rules were enforced by sixth formers, who had the power to "sting hours," that is, assign manual work around campus lasting for an hour or more. Working off hours in the barn was a harsh penalty, and may have produced an unexpected outcome. One morning, we showed up for job assembly—the daily school-wide meeting—to find evidence that a cow had been in the auditorium. The identity of the rustlers was revealed years later—too late for disciplinary action—by a photograph in our senior yearbook.

We not only ate at the same time, we went to class, study hall, chapel, and bed at the same time. There were class periods Saturday morning, but not Wednesday afternoon, to allow for mid-week and weekend interscholastic athletic events. On weekday afternoons, everyone participated in intramural sports or varsity practices, coached by faculty. Father Sill, a coxswain on the Columbia University crew during his undergraduate years, chose the site for his school on the Housatonic River partly to indulge his love of rowing.[6] Kent crews have dominated interscholastic rowing since the early years. The boys' first boat won the national championship most recently in 2010 and the girls' first boat won in 2015. I signed up for crew in my third form year, but after nearly catching a crab—crew-speak for being ejected from the shell by an errant oar—I switched to tennis. I played varsity football in the fall and basketball in the winter. The football coach awarded me a letter ("K"), believing that any boy who attended practice and games deserved the honor. The basketball coach did not, believing that performance, not participation, was the proper criteria. This was my introduction to the difference between democracy and meritocracy.

Being on a varsity team allowed travel to other schools but unless a parent came to visit on a weekend afternoon, no one could venture off campus. When my parents visited during my third and fourth form years, they would drive five miles up Skiff Mountain to observe construction of the Kent Girls School campus. In 1961, the first class of girls was admitted as fifth-formers. The class of 1963, of which I am a member, was the first to graduate both males and females. Each school had its own headmaster, faculty, and classes. Some faculty taught and some students attended classes on both campuses, an arrangement known as coordinate education. Socializing occurred at sporting events, movies, concerts, and some co-curricular activities, facilitated by buses that shuttled between campuses. Socializing did not include kissing, an offense punishable by sixty-days in supervised study hall.

Progress toward gender diversity was not matched by rigorous attempts to implement racial and ethnic diversity until much later. My class of sixty-two boys included one Asian - American and two African - American boys. Classmates from outside the United States were typically sons of American parents living abroad. One exception was our English exchange student, who went on to become the head of the British Secret Intelligence Service. To foster economic diversity,

Kent School
The Author 1962

however, Father Sill had implemented a "sliding scale" of tuition payments, under which wealthier families, in effect, subsidized poorer families. A strict dress code—jackets and ties, dress pants, and shoes—and an allowance of $0.80 per week were intended to counteract social class distinction. We chose a roommate and changed rooms once a year. Dorm rooms contained bunk beds, a wardrobe, and two desks with gang toilets down the hall. The call of "heads up" was frequently heard in the showers when someone flushed a toilet.

These words from the school song still conjure up the beauty of the place for me: "the haze on Algo's height is rent, morning unsheathes

PREFACE

its fiery sword, the lovely land of Kent, comes forth in light to hail her Lord." The campus is nestled between Mount Algo and the Housatonic River. The changing seasons inspire my most vivid memories of the place. "October belongs to God," William Armstrong, a long term-faculty member, once declared. The fall foliage displayed on Algo's mountainside does indeed provide a reverential backdrop for the green lawns and blue waters of the valley campus. Winter, however, belonged to snow and ice. Hockey players braved the frigid temperature to skate on a frozen pond. We dreaded the trek from our dorms to the dining hall for breakfast accompanied by the unappetizing aroma of cow dung in the frosty air. When river ice began to crack and floes started to rumble downriver, we knew the arrival of spring was imminent.[7] Spring meant regattas, dance weekend, hikes to numeral rock,[8] and wardrobe change: Bass Weejuns (no socks, ever), madras shorts (preferably faded and wrinkled), polo shirt (collar up and untucked, even then), and a blue blazer (with crest).

The elegant buildings match the beauty of the natural setting. The exterior design of the dormitories and classroom buildings is uniformly Georgian Revival: red brick walls, mullioned windows, white painted woodwork, and slate roofs with dormers. The all-stone chapel and bell tower and the headmaster's house—designed in the 1950s by a former headmaster in the style of Frank Lloyd Wright—are notable exceptions. The spatial quality of the chapel interior—stone floor, unadorned stone walls, one dazzling stained-glass window, and a timber-framed roof infused with incense from years of worship services—resonates with me whenever I return.

My Kent School experience was not unlike that of my classmates and of my contemporaries at other boarding schools. Kent's demographics, curriculum, and world-view, however, have changed with the times. In 1992, after an eight-year planning process, Kent consolidated the two schools on the valley campus. Chapel attendance is still required, but only two evenings a week. The curriculum, while still centered on the liberal arts, now offers expanded choices in addition to core requirements: more lab science courses, a pre-engineering program, electives, advanced placement, and independent study; all supported by academic advising. While fewer graduates are accepted at Ivy League universities, they enjoy wider choices to find the college that is right for them. Financial aid grants, enabled by a growing endowment, replaced the sliding tuition scale as a means of maintaining economic diversity. There is no longer a second form (eighth grade), but incoming students may matriculate at any level, including a post-graduate year. There are more day students, but they comprise less than ten percent of the student body. Newer dormitories and renovated older ones contain common rooms and provide two separate beds in each room. Meals are less formal with flexible hours, seating arrangements, and menu choices. While kitchen staff now handle dishwashing, students still perform daily jobs. Despite these changes, the lovely valley land of Kent and *Temperantia, Fiducia, Constantina* are still part of the school's DNA . . . and mine.

Notes

1 - The "whole student" is a term popularized by educational progressives in the early twentieth - century, based on European educational theorists including Jean-Jacques Rousseau and John Heinrich Pestalozzi.

2 - *American Education a history* page 83.

3 - My younger brother graduated from Kent five years after I did, but we had significantly different experiences.

4 - Unless noted otherwise, dates in parentheses after a person's name indicate tenure in an official position.

5 - *Kent One Hundred Years* page 27.

6 - ibid. page 1.

7 - In January 2018, a mile-long ice dam formed on the Housatonic River adjacent to the Kent School campus. Flooding of buildings and roadways and disruption of basic infrastructure closed the school for almost two weeks. Students and teachers continued their coursework by e-mail, chat rooms, Skype, and other electronic media.

8 - Numeral Rock is an outcropping near the summit of Mount Algo. Fifth-formers paint their graduating class numerals on the rock in the spring before their sixth-form year. The rock is visible for miles around.

Brandford Academy
Built 1820

1: EDUCATION OF YOUTH IN AMERICA

As to their Studies, it would be well if they could be taught every Thing which is useful, and every Thing that is ornamental; But Art is long, and their Time is short.

Benjamin Franklin, 1749[1]

THIS BOOK EXAMINES THE HERITAGE, values, and aspirations of a select group of private, college preparatory, boarding schools (prep schools) belonging to the Eight Schools Association—Choate Rosemary Hall, Deerfield Academy, The Hotchkiss School, The Lawrenceville School, Northfield Mount Hermon School, Phillips Academy Andover, Phillips Exeter Academy, and St. Paul's School—through the lens of campus planning and architecture. To place the development of these schools in context, this chapter traces the evolution of public elementary and secondary education in America.

PURPOSE AND PEDAGOGY

For generations parents, educators, and politicians have struggled to achieve a balance between the laboring (specialized skills) and the learned (intellectual growth), between traditional and progressive attitudes toward teaching and learning, between the elite and the masses, between local and central control, between secular and religious, and between public and private support.

The first European settlers on the North American continent placed high value on educating their children. Survival, both short-term and future, depended on the first generation's ability to transmit their cultural values and living skills to their children. For the New England Puritan in the 1600s, such as Cotton Mather and his ancestors, literacy—the ability to read the bible and apply its lessons to daily life—was essential to counteract the temptations of the "old deluder" Satan.[2] Benjamin Franklin—whose abilities ranged from operator of a printing press to Ambassador to France—saw the need to provide an education that was as once useful (practical) and ornamental (cultured). Samuel Phillips, Jr.—founder of Phillips Academy Andover in Massachusetts in 1778—believed a student should learn "the great end and real business of living."[3] Thomas Jefferson—primary author of the Declaration of Independence—promoted an educated citizenry who could understand and practice the tenets of a democratic society. Emma Willard—founder of a girls secondary school in 1821—advocated a "Republican Motherhood" by which future mothers could provide a moral compass for their sons who would become the nation's leaders.[4] At the same time, Yale president Jeremiah Day reported his faculty's belief that education was intended to discipline and furnish the mind.[5] Horace Mann—"the patron saint of public education"—in the 1830s advocated the inclusive character and social purpose of the common school.[6] At the turn of the twentieth century, John Dewey—"the father of progressive education"—wanted to develop the social, intellectual, emotional, and physical parts of the whole child.[7] W. E. B. DuBois—author of *The Souls of Black Folk* published in 1903—advocated that the "talented tenth" of his race should be educated, not trained.[8] William A. Wirt—superintendent of schools in Gary, Indiana, in the first decade of the twentieth century—believed manual training would help assimilate immigrants and preserve the American way of life.[9] Charles Kingsley, a teacher who articulated The Cardinal Principals of Secondary Education in a 1918 report, saw the educational system as a social and vocational sorting mechanism.[10] After World War II, Arthur Bestor, university professor and author, promoted a return to a liberal arts education with less specialization.[11] Lyndon B. Johnson, president of the United States in the 1960s, used education as a tool to reduce poverty, combat racism, and ensure equal opportunity. Bill Gates, founder of Microsoft and philanthropist, advocates a "common core" to prepare students to succeed in college and to promote digital literacy. Following is a detailed look at issues identified in this chronology.

TUTORS, GRAMMAR SCHOOLS, AND MISSIONARY SCHOOLS: 1630s THROUGH 1770s[12]

Education in the American colonies can be characterized as informal and inconsistent, ad-hoc and as-needed. If a parent or relative were literate, a child's early education would likely take place in the home. If not, or in addition, a child might attend a "dame school" in which local women taught basic reading. Other neighbors, mainly men, taught writing, focused on useful skills like penmanship (scribes) and book keeping (clerks). Church elders and pastors might provide more advanced lessons using the New England Primer and focusing on learning the Protestant catechism. Families with higher ambitions for their children and the means to pursue them employed a tutor. Some tutors, like Philip Fithian of Virginia, lived with a family. Between 1773 and 1774, Fithian tutored Robert Carter's family of seven children, ranging in age from four to seventeen, in subjects from letters to Latin. Others, such as the Reverend James Maury, ran "parson's schools." Among Maury's students were George Washington, Thomas Jefferson, James Madison, and James Monroe, four of the first five presidents of the United States.

While tutors educated a small number of children from affluent families, grammar schools were the preferred setting to prepare young men for college. The curriculum included Greek, Latin, Hebrew, geography, history, and basic mathematics, all required for college entrance. By the beginning of the Revolutionary War, there were nine colleges in the colonies, beginning with Harvard, which was founded in 1636.[13] The Massachusetts General School Law of 1647 (aka the Old Deluder Satan Act) required towns of more than one hundred households to establish a grammar school "to instruct youth so far as they may be fitted for the university."[14] Because of a shortage of qualified students, some colleges ran grammar schools. In 1749 Benjamin Franklin published his *Proposals Relating to the Education of Youth in Pensilvania*. Based on these proposals, he founded the Academy and Charitable School, the progenitor of the University of Pennsylvania. One of Franklin's more innovative and controversial proposals was that instruction would be conducted in English, rather than Latin.

Part of the mission of the Puritans (today's Congregationalists) and later other denominations including Presbyterians and Anglicans (today's Episcopalians) was to bring Christianity to Native Americans, the unschooled, and the unchurched. Harvard College built an Indian College on its Cambridge, Massachusetts, campus in 1655 and some years later published an Algonquin language bible. In 1743 Rev. Eleazar Wheelock founded a charity school—later named Moor's College—in Columbia, Connecticut, to train Native American youth as missionaries. In 1769, Wheelock received a royal charter and funding to move Moor's College to Hanover, New Hampshire. He reestablished his earlier college preparatory academy, and named the combined schools Dartmouth College to honor Lord Dartmouth, the college's chief benefactor. By the 1770s, the Anglican Society for the Propagation of the Gospel in Foreign Parts had established approximately 170 "charity schools" in the colonies teaching elementary reading, writing, and arithmetic and the Protestant catechism to children of poor families and Native Americans.

By the time of the Revolutionary War, approximately 90 percent of male and 60 percent of female American colonists were considered literate, as defined by the ability to sign one's name.

ACADEMIES: 1770S THROUGH 1820S[15]

After the British surrender and the ratification of the Constitution, Americans sought to establish their identity as a nation. One means to this end was to purge British grammar and pronunciation from American elementary schools. In 1783–5, Noah Webster—known later as "the schoolmaster of the republic"—published a series of textbooks written from an American and a secular perspective. The first, a book known as the "blue-backed speller," was followed by grammar and reader textbooks. The speller was widely used—over 15 million copies were sold by 1837—and was the precursor of Webster's *An American Dictionary of the English Language,* published in 1828.

Thomas Jefferson, another champion of public education, believed that ignorance was the enemy of democracy. He introduced a "Bill for the more general diffusion of knowledge" in the Virginia legislature to establish a tax-supported public school system, but it failed to pass several times between 1779 and 1817. After his term as U.S. president (1801–1809), he channeled his vision and energy into creating a state university.

Noah Webster, 1886
The School Master of the Republic

This time the government supported him. Between 1818 and 1824, Jefferson, working with a state commission, designed the campus and buildings as well as the curriculum of the University of Virginia.

The academy became the vehicle for achieving Webster's and Jefferson's goals. The nineteenth-century academy is roughly the equivalent of today's high school. Latin grammar schools prepared students headed for college, but the academies served both this need—via the Classical curriculum—and the needs of students headed for the workplace—via the English curriculum. Some academies were tax supported, others tuition and donor supported, and some a combination of the two. Most were boys only, some were girls only—such as Emma Willard's Troy Female Seminary—and some were coeducational. By 1850, there were approximately 6,000 academies in the country, with a corresponding decline in the number of Latin grammar schools. Four of the eight schools in this book were founded in this era: Phillips Academy Andover in 1778; Phillips Exeter Academy in 1781; Deerfield Academy in 1797; and Maidenhead Academy, later

Catherine Beecher, 1848

renamed The Lawrenceville School, in 1810.

The academies, especially those offering the English curriculum, gradually introduced scientific study to their coursework. Inspiration came from accomplishments such as the transcontinental Lewis and Clark expedition. President Jefferson commissioned the Corps of Discovery in 1803, partly to find an inland water route to the Pacific Ocean as a conduit for commerce, but also to conduct scientific research. Prior to embarking, Meriwether Lewis spent a year in Philadelphia learning the rudiments of astronomy for surveying and map making, medicine for treating disease and injury, and natural science to document and collect plant, animal, and fossil specimens.

Beginning with the colonial colleges, institutions of higher learning have led the way for secondary school curricula. The U.S. Military Academy at West Point, New York, founded in 1802, became "a national center for science study." Rensselaer Polytechnic Institute in Troy, New York, founded in 1824, was known as "the center for applied science in the United States." Practical applications of scientific discovery—such as bridges, canals, tunnels, and steam locomotion—appealed to families who were not necessarily interested in educating their children in the traditional Classical manner.

COMMON SCHOOLS: 1820s THROUGH 1850s[16]

The first six presidents of the United States were gentry from Virginia or Massachusetts. However, the presidential election of 1827 elevated a "common man" to the highest level of government. That man was Andrew Jackson from Tennessee. Jackson, and his successor Martin van Buren, served for twelve years, during which educators reformed elementary level schooling (first through eighth grade) to provide universal access, a uniform curriculum, and professional teachers. These reforms constituted the "common school." Catharine Beecher founded the Hartford Female Seminary in 1823 to prepare teachers for these schools. Having succeeded in Connecticut, she founded additional teacher's schools in the Midwest over the next twenty years. Horace Mann—the Massachusetts Secretary of Education from 1837 to 1848—succeeded in promoting common school reforms and creating a tax-supported public school system, a move that other states soon adopted. During his tenure, Mann visited and assessed almost every school district in Massachusetts. He held town meetings to persuade parents and educators to adopt his reforms.

Common schools were ostensibly non-racist and non-sectarian. Massachusetts abolished racial segregation in schools in 1855, but for a century, segregation was condoned in

Common School Classroom Replica

schools and public facilities nationwide. In the 1850s, Roman Catholics, offended by the overwhelming Protestant bias in the common school curriculum, established a parochial school system for their children. In New York City, Catholic bishops argued for public funding of the parochial schools, but in 1875, New York State ruled that public funds could not be used for private schools.[17]

An 1827 Massachusetts law mandated that towns of more than 500 families support a secondary school in addition to a public elementary school. Boston Girl's High and Normal School opened in 1852, and by 1856, there were approximately 140 high schools in the country, mostly in large cities. Philadelphia, for example, had opened Central High in 1838. These public schools were in direct competition with private grammar schools and academies. They were not only free, but offered both the Classical and English curricula.

HIGH SCHOOLS: 1860s THROUGH 1900s[18]

Immigration and industrialization changed the demographics of eastern and midwestern cities and impacted their public schools. New York City's population, for example, grew from 81,000 in 1800 to 1.2 million by 1860, and 3.4 million by 1900. The first wave of immigrants came primarily from England and Holland, the second wave from Ireland and Germany, and the third wave from southern and eastern Europe. Each ethnic group brought its language and culture putting a burden on schools to "Americanize" the children of the first generation.

In contrast to voluntary immigration, more than ten million African natives were forcibly brought to North and South America as slaves from the sixteenth to mid-nineteenth century.[19] During the U.S. Civil War, more than four million slaves were emancipated. Like free blacks in the Union states, these former slaves saw schooling as a way to ensure their freedom. They found themselves, however, in racially seg-

American Progress,
1872
John Gast

regated, generally inferior schools. In 1896, the U.S. Supreme Court upheld school segregation provided that predominantly black schools were equal to predominantly white schools.

Industrialization created jobs for workers and fortunes for investors, but unfortunately many workers were children. To counteract this abuse, states passed laws restricting child labor and making school attendance mandatory for children under fourteen years old. As a result, in 1870, the nation's public elementary and secondary (high) schools enrolled over 7.6 million students. By 1890, that number grew to 12.7 million. To accommodate the changed demographics and increased population of the cities, educators devised the "one best system." This system imposed standardization and hierarchal organization on the schools. Grade levels were assigned by age, a uniform course of study was developed, and district-wide testing measured performance.

In reaction to negative urban living conditions, some wealthy families moved to newly developed suburbs, such as Brookline near Boston, Tuxedo Park near New York City, and the Main Line communities near Philadelphia. Private boarding schools offered another option for urban families. Four of the eight schools in this book were founded during this era: St. Paul's School in 1856, Mount Hermon in 1881 (later merged with Northfield Seminary for Young Ladies, founded in 1879), The Hotchkiss School in 1891, and Choate in 1896 (later merged with Rosemary Hall, a girl's school founded in 1890).

As the second and third waves of European immigrants arrived on the eastern seaboard, many Americans of prior generations migrated west. The concept of "manifest destiny," first articulated by New York journalist John O'Sullivan, portrayed western migration as inexorable and redemptive. In 1893, historian Frederick Jackson Turner published his thesis arguing that the moving frontier was a generative and defining concept. Despite these high concepts, as settlers moved west, Native American's lands were seized and tribes forced onto reservations. Andrew Jackson's Indian Removal Act of 1830 had precipitated this practice. Those who empathized with native American children established off-reservation boarding schools such as the prototypical Carlisle Indian School in Pennsylvania. These schools were intended to assimilate native Americans and make them fit for American citizenship.

The settlers established rural schools, such as the ones portrayed in Laura Ingalls Wilder's *Little House on the Prairie* series. The stories are fictionalized versions of her own experience as a child in a pioneer family between 1871 and 1885 in Wisconsin and the Dakota territories. She portrayed Laura as six years old and her sister Mary as eight years old attending a one-room schoolhouse with one teacher. At age eighteen, Laura secures her first job as teacher in Common School #6, a graded elementary school in North Dakota.

Higher education also underwent a transformation in this era. The Morill land grant acts of 1862 and 1890 allowed states to sell Federal land in the west and use the proceeds to fund public agricultural and mining (A&M) colleges and normal (teacher training) schools. As public high schools became prevalent, colleges closed their preparatory departments and developed graduate and professional schools. The College of New Jersey celebrated its 150th anniversary in 1896, started a graduate school, and was renamed Princeton University. The undergraduate college, either freestanding or part of a university, became the domain of the liberal arts curriculum. The first liberal arts colleges for women were founded, beginning with Vassar College in 1861.[20] Cornell, a recipient of land grant funds, was founded as a university in 1868, and Johns Hopkins was founded primarily as a graduate school in 1886.

PROGRESSIVE ERA: 1890s THROUGH 1940s [21]

In secondary school education, the progressive movement influenced both pedagogy and administration. Most influential of the progressive educators was John Dewey, a professor of Philosophy and head the Department of Education at the University of Chicago. He and his followers believed in child-centered pedagogy rather than the dominance of teachers and textbooks. This belief coincided with a new awareness of childhood as a unique stage of development. Heretofore, children had been treated as little adults. In practice, Dewey's theory involved learning by doing: manual training, physical exercise, and study of a variety of subjects based on a child's interest.

Meanwhile, administrative progressives applied a corporate and military model of management to school systems. The chain of command flowed from the state department of education to the local school district board of education, superintendent of schools, school principals, and, finally, teachers. Teachers, administrators, and educational foundations established national organizations to promulgate standards and promote their interests. Schools administered newly developed intelligence quota (IQ) tests to develop student profiles. By the 1940s, the College Board, founded in 1900, became the gatekeeper of college admissions by administering the universal SATs (scholastic aptitude, and later, achievement tests).

Character building and socialization remained part of the educational landscape, but in newly developed forms. Scouting, for both boys and girls, the YMCA (men) and the YWCA (women) taught citizenship and leadership skills as well as outdoor survival skills and recreational sports. Scholastic athletics became part of the curricular and extracurricular offerings. Urban organizations, such as New York City's Public

Schools Athletic League, provided an alternative to street gangs and delinquent behavior. Beginning in 1917, an annual national scholastic basketball tournament was held. Blacks and Catholics were excluded, but these groups organized their own tournaments. The movie *Hoosiers* is a vivid portrayal of civic and personal values found in high school athletics in the 1950s.

By 1910, there were approximately 10,000 public high schools nationwide, compared with about 500 in the 1870s. In the 1930s, the mandatory attendance age was raised to sixteen and by the 1950s, approximately eighty percent of all eligible high schools students were enrolled. The increasing numbers and diversity of the student population led Charles Kingsley to articulate The Cardinal Principals of Secondary Education, which, in essence, stated the purpose of a high school education was to prepare students for their adult lives. Combining the values of common with individualized schooling, the comprehensive high school became the vehicle to achieve this purpose. A comprehensive high school offers three tracks: academic for students who intend to go to college, commercial for students who intend to pursue business careers, and vocational for students who intend to work in the trades.

World Wars One and Two and the Great Depression had a major impact on education. After World War One, approximately 1 million blacks migrated from the rural south to the urban north and Mid-west to seek employment and education. The depression caused dramatic social dislocation, poverty, and cutbacks in school funding. World War Two drew young men to the military and young women to factories. After the war, men had the opportunity to attend college through the G.I. Bill and women gained independence from the roles of housewife and mother. These societal changes became more intense in the succeeding decades.

LIBERATION ERA: 1950s THROUGH 1980s [22]

Civil rights and civic unrest were the hallmarks of American society and education during the 1950s–1980s. The federal government assumed an activist role to create equal opportunity for disadvantaged minorities, women, and persons with disabilities. The Supreme Court declared segregation unconstitutional in the landmark case Brown vs. Board of Education of Topeka in 1954. Shortly after, Governor Orval Faubus of Arkansas dramatized this sea change when he tried to prevent black students from entering a previously all-white high school. A few years later, Governor George Wallace tried to prevent black students from entering an auditorium at the University of Alabama. In both cases, presidential orders authorized local national guards to enforce the law.

Title IX of the 1972 Education Amendment Act made sex discrimination illegal in schools and colleges receiving federal funds. Among other gains, this law changed the character of athletics and the facilities that supported them. In this period, although not compelled by statute, heretofore private, all-male colleges began admitting women. In the 1970s, the federal government—in a precursor to the Americans with Disabilities Act of 1990—withheld federal funds from schools that were found to discriminate against children with disabilities.

In the late 1960s, disillusioned and rebellious youth, primarily of high school and college age, coalesced into the counterculture whose mantras included "tune in, turn on, drop out." The assassinations of President John F. Kennedy, his brother Robert, and Martin Luther King Jr.—together with the prospect of a nuclear winter—contributed to the general sense of alienation and despair. Demonstrations against U.S. involvement in the Vietnam War disrupted campuses, and, in some cases, caused arson and deaths. Environmental activists created public awareness of the causes and effects of water and air pollution, clear-cutting forests, mountaintop removal to mine coal, species extermination, and other abuses. The first world-wide Earth Day was held in 1970.

Disruption on the campus carried over into the classroom. The federal government's response to the 1957 Russian launch of the satellite Sputnik was to provide massive funding for public education, particularly in math, science, foreign languages, teacher training, and school construction. In 1969, Apollo 11, the first manned moon landing, salvaged America's reputation as a world leader in science. Conduct of the Cold War insured that funding for scientific research would continue unabated. President Lyndon B. Johnson, as part of his "War on Poverty," prodded congress to approve four billion dollars for pre-school education (Head Start), bilingual education (later English as a second language or ESL), and other programs to promote quality and equality in the public schools.

SCHOOL CHOICE: 1980s TO THE PRESENT [23]

The impact of electronic technology and the school choice movement began in the early 1980s and continues to this day. Main frame computers evolved into personal electronic devices, and centralized school governance evolved into a scholastic marketplace. Just as the Cold War incentivized the federal government to fund scientific research, global economic competition motivated the corporate sector to undertake educational reform. Advances in astrophysics, molecular biology, high-speed computing, and the insertion of the internet into every facet of human interaction were adapted for schools in the form of the integrated STEM (science, technology, engineering, and math) curriculum. Global warming, as well as the stockpile of nuclear weapons, threatens the existence of life on earth as we know it. Sustainability—the means to reduce greenhouse gas emissions and conserve natural resources—is embedded in building codes as well as school curricula.

The concentration of wealth in Asian nations and in the bank accounts of the America's "one percent" increases the possibility of class and global conflict. U.S. private schools and colleges are opening facilities in Asia, and Asian students are enrolling in American private schools colleges in record numbers.[24] Immigration of Asian and Hispanic families is changing the face of American public school classrooms. Global terrorism, such as the 9/11 attacks, and domestic terrorism, such as school shootings in Columbine and Newtown, have made security a top priority.

Against the backdrop of these global and national cataclysms, school reform has been a continuing battle since the Reagan administration (1981–1989). In 1983, a presidential commission issued a report titled "A Nation at Risk," citing foreign competition as a wake-up call for school reform. This report encouraged corporations to apply free market principals—competition, choice, and accountability—to education. One response was a hybrid public-private school known as a charter school. Charter schools are tax supported—except for buildings—charge no tuition, and are open to all, but they sidestep local school boards. They are governed by state

Keystone Academy, rendering
Beijing, China

charter and are run either by not-for-profit organizations—parent, religious, or community—or by for-profit companies. Minnesota chartered the first of these schools in 1991, and by 2014 there were over 6,800 state chartered schools in the country. Controversy has surrounded the charter school movement because of the use of vouchers and tax credits that some believe constitute the use of public funds for private purposes. Edison Schools, a for-profit company hired to manage public and charter schools in the 1990s, backed away from this role when cost was found to be higher, and performance lower, than comparable public schools. Another response, the magnet school, was initially created as an alternative to government mandated busing as a means to integrate schools in the 1970s. Today, that purpose has been subsumed under the rubric "school choice." Magnet schools are part of a local public school system, but students are not limited to the school nearest their home. Admission is theoretically open to all, but when the number of applicants exceeds the number of available places, a selection process, a lottery for example, is employed. A magnet school typically emphasizes a particular curriculum—for example performing arts—and/or a particular pedagogy—Montessori method, for example. The 1980 film *Fame* fictionalized life at the High School of Performing Arts in New York City, a prototypical magnet school. By 2011, there were over 2,700 magnet schools nationwide.

Whether public, private, or hybrid, schools are integrating online learning in their pedagogy. Digital instruction, the internet, and tablets are the new slide projector, chalkboard, and textbook. In blended learning programs, students complete courses both in the classroom and at home using online resources. School districts can purchase supplemental online coursework from vendors or from state "virtual schools." Ohio, a leader in online learning, adopted the

Memorial Hall Museum (formerly The Academy Building of 1799)

charter school model to distribute course content through distance learning. Distance learning has accelerated the home schooling trend and augmented school based professional development for teachers. Florida offers a full-time, online, elementary and secondary school education.

Looking back at the evolution of secondary school education, it is clear that private, college preparatory boarding schools faced many of the same forces and challenges as public high schools. The next section, a case study of Deerfield Academy, shows the intertwined relationship of public and private schools.

FROM PUBLIC TO PRIVATE:
DEERFIELD ACADEMY

To tell the story of Deerfield Academy is in part to tell the story of American education in the nineteenth and twentieth centuries and to tell of the town itself. [25] Linus Travers, Class of 1954

English settlers founded Deerfield—a town in Massachusetts on the Deerfield River in the Pocumtuck valley—in the 1670s. The town barely survived a lethal attack by French and Native American warriors in 1704 and remained contested until the late 1740s. In 1797, town leaders formed a corporation and obtained a charter from the commonwealth to establish an academy. The trustees raised funds from donors and bond sales, hired a preceptor, purchased an acre of land, and erected a school building. The Academy Building, now used as a museum, was designed by Asher Benjamin, one of America's first professional architects. The academy opened in 1799 with a population of thirty-nine boys and eight girls. Nineteen of the students lived in Deerfield and the rest boarded with families in town during the school year. The curriculum included a Classical (college preparatory) track and an English (general education) track. By 1826, enrollment had grown to thirty-eight girls and

Deerfield High School and Deerfield Academy, 1878

thirty-seven boys.

In 1858, the town of Deerfield was sued for failure to comply with the 1827 Massachusetts statute requiring towns of more than 500 households to provide a secondary (high) school. The town government and academy trustees subsequently established a joint high school and academy. The town provided financial support and non-resident students paid tuition. In 1875, a bequest from the estate of Esther Dickinson for a "free high school and library" enabled construction of a new building—designed by the prominent Boston architectural firm Peabody & Stearns[26]—for the reorganized Dickinson High School and Deerfield Academy.

By 1902, enrollment in Deerfield Academy, the repository of the classical curriculum, had dwindled to fourteen students. Frank L. Boyden,[27] a recent Amherst College graduate and the new headmaster of the academy, successfully raised money, recruited students, and hired faculty. By 1920, he had the resources to build a forty-student dormitory and renovate several seventeenth-century houses for academy purposes. Another crisis arose when Massachusetts ruled that public funds could not be used for private purposes, a ruling that threatened the town-academy alliance. In 1923, with funds raised from Amherst alumni and benefactors of Exeter and several other private schools, the academy purchased its share of the joint high school and academy. Reorganized as a private, college preparatory boarding school, Deerfield Academy thrived under Boyden's tenure, which extended to 1968.

SUMMARY

Private, college preparatory, boarding schools are a small subset of the approximately 33,000 independent secondary schools in the United States. The number of students attending independent schools is less than ten percent of those attending the nation's almost 132,000 public and charter schools.[28] The residential character of boarding schools, however, distinguishes them from independent day schools and public schools. The need for dormitories, dining halls, student centers, and faculty housing—in addition to academic and athletic facilities—creates the opportunity to develop a campus. Campus planning produces a functional and aesthetic composition of buildings and grounds. Individual buildings create the opportunity for architectural expression. The following chapters examine the themes introduced in this chapter through their influence on the design of the campuses and buildings of the Eight Schools Association.

Notes

Brief biographies are included the first time a person or organization is mentioned in the text.

1 - *Proposals relating to the education of youth in Pensilvania.*

2 - *American Education*, page 45.

3 - *After the Harkness Gift*, page 8.

4 - *Wrought with Stedfast Will*, page 44.

5 - *The American College and University*, page 132.

6 - *School, the story of American public education*, page 31.

7 - ibid. page 77.

8 - *American Education*, page 176.

9 - *School, the story of American public education*, pages 78–89; "the goal of manual training was to make every working man a scholar, and every scholar a working man."

10 - *American Education*, page 272.

11 - *School, the story of American public education*, page 115.

12 - Background for this section is *School, the story of American public education* and *American Education: the Colonial experience*.

13 - The other colonial colleges (in order of founding dates) are: The College of William and Mary, Yale College, The College of Philadelphia (later Pennsylvania), The College of New Jersey (later Princeton), King's College (later Columbia), Dartmouth College, Queen's College (later Rutgers), and The College of Rhode Island (later Brown).

14 - *American Education: the Colonial experience*, page 45. The intended "university" was Harvard, although it was still a college.

15 - The background for this section is *American Education: the Colonial experience* and *The American College and University*. General Sylvanus Thayer, superintendent of the U.S. Military Academy from 1817 to 1833, also funded a professional school of engineering at Dartmouth College in 1867–71 and, through his estate, a college preparatory academy in Braintree, Massachusetts.

16 - The background for this section is *American Education: the Colonial experience* and *School, the story of American public education*.

17 - A proposed amendment to the U.S. Constitution prohibiting the use of public funds for private schools failed to pass Congress.

18 - The background for this section is *American Education: the Colonial experience; School, the story of American public education;* and *The American College and University*.

19 - *Worlds together, worlds apart*, page 495.

20 - Other women's colleges founded in this era include: Radcliffe, Smith, Wellesley, Bryn Mawr, Barnard, and Mount Holyoke.

21 - The background for this section is *American Education* and *School, the story of American public education*.

22 - ibid.

23 - The background for this section is *American Education: the Colonial experience; School, the story of American public education; Common Sense, The New York Times Magazine*, February 26, 2017, pages 13–15; and *Keeping Pace with K-12 Digital Learning, twelfth edition 2015*, the Evergreen Education Group.

24 - Keystone Academy—a K-12 private, college preparatory, boarding and day school in Beijing, China, that opened in 2014—was founded by Malcolm McKenzie, former Head of The Hotchkiss School, and Edward Shanahan, former head of Choate Rosemary Hall.

25 - *Deerfield 1797–1997*, page 7.

26 - Peabody & Stearns (active 1870s to 1910s) designed academic buildings at Smith, Harvard, Groton, Andover, Middlesex, and new campus for Lawrenceville in 1880s. Peabody embraced several architectural styles, including Colonial Revival and Queen Anne.

27 - Frank Learoyd Boyden was the headmaster of Deerfield Academy for sixty-six years (1902–1968). He guided the school through the public-private transition in the first decades of the twentieth century, and elevated the academy to the highest ranks of private, college preparatory, boarding schools.

28 - National Association of Independent Schools (NAIS), 2017 data.

The Lawrenceville School
Bunn Memorial Library

2: THE WHOLE STUDENT: TEACHING AND LEARNING

Dr. McCosh was interested in secondary education, and with many others was working to secure a school in New Jersey that would do for Princeton what Andover, Exeter and St. Paul's, recently founded, were doing for Harvard and Yale.
        Roland Mulford, *History of the Lawrenceville School 1810–1935*

Dr. James McCosh was president of the College of New Jersey—now Princeton University—when he expressed this goal in his 1878 commencement address at the Lawrenceville Classical and Commercial High School, now The Lawrenceville School. Timothy Dwight, president of Yale College, went a step further. In 1885, he persuaded Mary Bissell Hotchkiss—a wealthy widow in Lakeville, Connecticut—to fund a secondary school that would prepare boys for college, in particular, Yale. Lawrenceville and Hotchkiss became "feeder schools" just as Andover was for Yale, and Exeter for Harvard. The appetite for Exeter graduates at Princeton, Yale, and Harvard was so large that it consumed almost two-thirds of Exeter's class of 1930. This close relationship between college preparatory schools and elite universities produced, among other valuable benefits for graduates, the "old boy" social and business network.

Another benefit of this relationship, also true for a wider range of high schools and colleges, is the academic leadership role assumed by the colleges and universities. When Harvard would revise its curriculum, and related admission requirements, the preparatory schools would follow.[1] In 1869, for example, Harvard president Charles Eliot introduced "useful subjects" including science, United States history, and modern languages. Shortly after, Exeter offered courses in these subjects, but not without resistance from Classics professors.[2] In the 1890s, a committee of Harvard professors established the Schools Examination Board to review the curricula and policies of selected college preparatory schools. The board visited schools and made recommendations that were in line with Harvard's expectations.[3] This review was a forerunner of the higher education accreditation process soon to be undertaken by the American Association of Universities. In 1945, Harvard faculty published *General Education in a Free Society* (the "Red Book") that advocated a core curriculum including English, history, modern languages, mathematics, science, and social studies, but not the classics.[4] The following year, at Exeter, Latin became an elective. In 1952, in a more direct collaboration, Exeter, Andover, and Lawrenceville—with Harvard, Yale and Princeton—developed standards for the Advanced Placement program. In 2009 The Graduate School of Education at the University of Pennsylvania established the UPenn Fellows program with a consortium of boarding schools including Deerfield, Hotchkiss, Lawrenceville, Northfield Mount Hermon, and St. Paul's.[5] This two-year residency program places Penn graduate students in one of the boarding schools to teach—under the guidance of a faculty mentor—coach, and live on campus for two years. The fellows and the schools of the consortium conduct joint conferences and share resources during the two-year term.

The following sections present examples of classrooms, libraries, science laboratories, and visual and performing arts spaces that reflect evolving curricula and pedagogy.

CLASSROOMS

Woodrow Wilson, while president of Princeton University, introduced the preceptorial method of teaching humanities to undergraduates. In 1907, the university built McCosh Hall, a classroom building that enabled his vision. Instead of large lecture halls and recitation rooms, there is a large number of smaller classrooms and offices for an expanded faculty, mostly junior members known as "preceptors." Several sizes of lecture halls are used according to enrollment in particular courses, but the key innovation was face to face discussion among students and a preceptor around a table. Wilson's vision was gradually adopted by other colleges and universities and eventually in some college preparatory schools.

Edward S. Harkness,[6] an heir to the Standard Oil fortune, had strong ideas about secondary school education. He donated much of his inheritance to advance teaching and research. Exeter was a principal beneficiary of his largess. Harkness had made gifts for faculty salaries and endowment in the 1920s, but in 1929 he challenged Exeter's principal, Lewis Perry,[7] to reimagine classroom teaching. Together they developed the "Harkness Plan" that followed very closely what Wilson had implemented at Princeton. Reducing class size to about twelve students each, meant more teachers and more opportunity for students and teachers to interact. This interaction extended to the dormitories, where a number of similarly sized groups, including a faculty adviser, would live and eat. This arrangement is known as the "house system." Harkness enabled this ambitious plan with over $5,800,000 in gifts over the next decade. Of this, $2,140,000 was dedicated to building a new classroom building, renovating teaching spaces in the Fourth Academy Building, building four new dormitories, and renovating eight others. Harkness also made smaller gifts for the same purpose to St. Paul's—his alma mater—Andover, Lawrenceville, and Taft, another New England college preparatory school. Harkness funds were also used to build residential colleges at Harvard and Yale.

Exeter's Fourth Academy Building is the academic center of the campus. As the name suggests, it had three predecessors. The first still exists on another site, and the second and third were destroyed by fire, unfortunately a common fate of many nineteenth-century school buildings. The current version was designed in 1915 by Cram and Ferguson, a Boston architectural firm headed by Ralph Adams Cram,[8] known for its work at the U.S. Military Academy and Princeton University. Whereas Cram designed these earlier buildings in his signature Collegiate Gothic style, he worked in a hybrid Georgian Revival-American Colonial style at Exeter. Cram sited the building facing a major town thoroughfare, but set back by a deep front lawn. He aligned the building in a row with earlier nineteenth-century school buildings. A Latin inscription in the lintel above over main entrance is translated "come here, boys, to be made men." After girls were admitted, another Latin phrase—translated "Here, boys and girls, seek goodness and knowledge" was inscribed above the existing one.[9]

Sixteen years after the Fourth Academy Building was constructed, Cram's firm renovated the building to accommodate the Harkness Plan. Cram also designed three additional buildings at this time—one academic, one administrative, and one residential—forming a courtyard on the opposite (south) side of the Academy Building. The primary goal of the renovation was to con-

Phillips Exeter Academy
Fourth Academy
Building

Phillips Exeter Academy,
Third Academy Building Classroom

Phillips Exeter Academy,
Harkness Classroom 1967

vert the second floor assembly hall, and large, fixed-seat lecture halls, into small seminar rooms. Cram designed an oval table for the rooms that allows all twelve or so students to face other rather than look at the backs of heads in a traditional assembly or lecture hall. The teacher sits with the students at the table, rather than standing on a platform behind a lectern. The "Harkness table" is evident today in classrooms where the conference, or tutorial, method is used. Over a span of twenty-seven years (1908–1935), Cram and Ferguson designed eighteen buildings for Exeter. As with Cass Gilbert at Hotchkiss Cram's long tenure and signature style define Exeter's public face.

THE WHOLE STUDENT: TEACHING AND LEARNING

St. Paul's School
Library Room

LIBRARIES

Books were the cultural capital of eighteenth-century America. Most colonial households owned a bible, but having a personal library conveyed erudition and status. John Harvard's gift of his library of about four hundred books in 1638 to the new college in the Massachusetts Bay Colony, was rewarded by having the college named for him. The Collegiate School, now Yale University, was founded in 1701 when ten congregational ministers pledged their support by donating their books. Benjamin Franklin—the founder of the College of Philadelphia, now the University of Pennsylvania—also founded The Library Company of Philadelphia, deemed by Franklin himself "The Mother of all the North American Subscription Libraries."[10] The early academies, and later the boarding schools, likewise ascribed high value to their book collections.

In the early years of an academy or school, a library would likely be housed in a room in the main academic building. When the collection grew and a donor emerged, the school would build a freestanding building. Over time, books began to crowd out readers. To rebalance the needs of books and readers, and to meet new requirements for fire-resistive construction and climate control, some schools renovated or replaced their earlier library buildings. In recent years, the advent of electronic resources caused another transformation of the traditional library. WiFi replaced the card catalogue and smartphones enable virtual browsing. Books remain, but a larger proportion of space is allocated to various needs of users, including lounge seating, tables, carrels, group-study rooms, and, in some cases, cafes.

St. Paul's School provides an example of this evolution. The school, founded in 1858, built its first classroom building in 1873 called "the Big Study." A room on the second floor functioned as the school library. By the turn of the twentieth-century, increased enrollment and course offerings had created demand for a purpose-built library. With a gift from the family of trustee William Sheldon, St. Paul's commissioned Ernest Flagg,[11] an architect trained at the Ecole des Beaux-Arts in Paris, to design the building. The school had selected a prominent and historic site on what became known as Library Pond. The pond, created by damming the Turkey River at a falls, served a mill in the eighteenth century.

Flagg's design features a recessed entry screened by four Tuscan columns, and a two-story, top-lit central reading room flanked by one story wings. The floor plan and massing follow Beaux Arts planning principals and resemble a scaled down version of Columbia University's Low Library built in 1897. The central block, however, is a tour-de-force Romanesque

St. Paul's School
Sheldon Library

Revival design transposed to turn of the twentieth-century New Hampshire: square in plan, four semicircular arches infilled with windows, low rise pyramidal roof clad in terra cotta tiles, and a cornice of copper and stone supported by muscular dentils. The exterior walls are roughcut, gray Concord granite with random coursing.

Sheldon Library served the school for almost ninety years.[12] In 1990, however, the trustee's decided to build a library for the twenty-first-century and hired Robert A. M. Stern Architects[13] to design the building. Once occupied by the Lower School, the Ohrstrom Library site is on a peninsula that straddles the Lower School Pond and the Library Pond. A pair of chapels, the smaller 1859 chapel and the magnificent 1886 chapel, share a greensward with the library. Stern's design responds to both site conditions, as well as the internal needs of a modern library. In a direct reference to H. H. Richardson's Crane Memorial Library, the floor plan is like a chapel: a long nave with book stacks in lieu of pews, an arched entrance at the transept, the main reading room in place of a choir and apse, and study areas in alcoves similar to side-aisle chapels.[14] The main double height reading room offers views of the Lower School Pond. The exterior masonry, bands of brick and sandstone, recalls the palette of the nineteenth-century chapels. For all the historic references, the library contains the electronic resources and user friendly features one expects in a twenty-first-century library.

Other notable Eight Schools libraries include Mellon Library (1926) at Choate Rosemary Hall, The Class of 1945 Library at Exeter (1971), and Bunn Library at Lawrenceville (1996). The Mellon Library contains bookstacks and reading rooms, but also classrooms, a conference center, publications offices, and dormitory rooms as part of the Hill House multi-use complex. The Class of 1945 Library at Exeter, designed by the eminent American architect Louis I. Kahn[15] received

THE WHOLE STUDENT: TEACHING AND LEARNING

St. Paul's School
Ohlstrom Library

the Twenty-Five Year Award—for buildings of lasting significance—from the American Institute of Architects in 1997. Bunn Library was designed by Graham Gund[16] of Boston in a post-modern style similar to Stern's Ohrstrom Library. See Chapter Eight for photographs and more about the architectural design of these buildings.

SCIENCE LABORATORIES

American education lagged behind the scientific revolution of sixteenth- and seventeenth-century Europe, and the industrial revolution of eighteenth and nineteenth century. In academia, Aristotle's "natural philosophy" was still in use as a synonym for science through the late nineteenth century. The Enlightenment view that nature and reason governed humankind's understanding of the universe came into conflict with the religious belief in the supernatural and the biblical revelation of truth. Some saw science as antithetical to religion while others saw science as religion's handmaiden, a debate that continues to this day. That the presidents of many private colleges and heads of private schools were clergymen well into the nineteenth century, likely slowed the acceptance of scientific coursework in the curriculum of their colleges and schools.

Following the groundbreaking efforts of Benjamin Franklin in Philadelphia, Joseph Henry at Princeton, and Benjamin Silliman at Yale, in the early nineteenth–century Union College and Rensselaer Institute of Technology instituted a "parallel" scientific curriculum. In mid-century the Lawrence Scientific School, affiliated with Harvard, and the Sheffield Scientific School, affiliated with Yale, accelerated the elevation of science and engineering as legitimate courses of study.[17] Once again, colleges led the preparatory schools.

Deerfield Academy provides an example of the gradual acceptance of science and engineering on par with the humanities. Some of the early proponents of scientific research and

Choate Rosemary Hall Lanphier Center

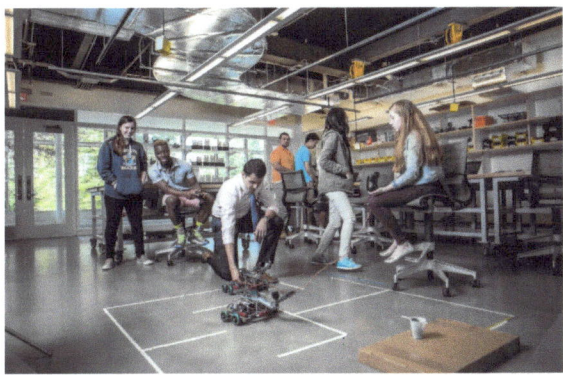

Choate Rosemary Hall, Lanphier Center Lab

teaching at Deerfield were women. Orra White was a preceptress of geology and astronomy between 1813 and 1818. She married an eminent Deerfield citizen and chemist, Edward Hitchcock, and moved with him to Amherst College when he became president. She continued her career as an illustrator of natural science, particularly botany and zoology.[18] Helen Childs, a graduate of Smith College, began her career as an instructor in math and science at Deerfield in 1905. Shortly after, she married Frank Boyden, the recently appointed headmaster, and continued teaching there until 1968.[19]

Jennie Arms Sheldon, an M.I.T. graduate and resident of Deerfield, donated funds in memory of her father to build Deerfield's first freestanding laboratory building. The Arms Science Building is located just north of the Main School Building facing the main street of Old Deerfield. Charles A. Platt,[20] principal of a Boston architectural firm, designed both buildings, Main in 1931 and Arms in 1933. Arms has two stories and a basement, and is crowned by a steep hipped roof. Four prominent chimneys—used to vent fumes—and tall windows—to illuminate high ceilinged labs within—suggest the function of the building. Otherwise the building conforms to the Colonial Revival style: red brick walls, symmetrically placed, but unadorned; windows; and a central entry featuring a semicircular portico supported by Ionic columns. When the Helen Childs Boyden Science Center opened in 1971, the academy re-purposed the building for humanities classrooms.

Deerfield Academy Arms Building (formerly science, currently humanities)

In the 1970s scientific coursework and teaching methods were in transition at colleges and secondary schools. The boundaries between the primary disciplines of physics, chemistry, and biology became porous, and interdisciplinary teaching and research was the trend. Lecture/demonstration teaching was replaced by hands-on experimentation. Main frame computers and punch cards were the precursors of electronic technology. The Boyden Science Center, designed by Robert Ward Jr. of Chicago, was the first example of modern architecture at Deerfield. It had an open plan, a low horizontal profile and, in one section, a flat roof. From delays during construction, to hostility to mid-century modern architecture, the building seemed doomed. It was demolished in 2006 to create a site for the Koch Center for Science, Math, and Technology.

Designed by Skidmore Owings and Merrill (SOM),[21] one of the largest architectural and engineering firms in the world, the Koch Center is free from historical references, unique in its multi-level massing, and at the leading edge of sustainable design. In addition to the basic sciences disciplines and mathematics classrooms, the program includes facilities for astronomical observation, independent research, computer science, and robotics. The building is also a social center, containing balconies, terraces, a cafe, and an atrium common space. It extends almost three hundred feet along the north side of the central campus green space and baseball diamond, and terraces down almost twenty feet to the lower level playing fields. The exterior elevations are unified by red/orange brick, but the massing is fragmented. Linear skylights separate the masses, bringing blue tinted light to the interior. Green roofs—planted with sedum for insulation and to capture rainwater—are intermixed with balconies and terraces. Curvilinear wall segments play

Deerfield Academy
Koch Science Center

off against rectangular planes.

Other notable Eight Schools science buildings include the Peabody Museum of Archaeology at Andover (1903) and the Lanphier Center for Mathematics and Computer Science at Choate Rosemary Hall (2015). The Kohler Environmental Center at Choate Rosemary Hall is featured in Chapter Six. The Peabody Museum, designed by Guy Lowell the campus architect at the time, is unique among college preparatory schools. No other school has an archaeological collection or a department and faculty to teach the subject. The Lanphier Center, designed by Pelli Clarke Pelli,[22] is connected by a bridge over a pond to the Icahn Center for Science designed by Pei Cobb Freed in 1989, completing a Science, Technology, Engineering, and Mathematics (STEM) complex. In 2007 Choate Rosemary Hall founded the Technology Learning Institute, a collaboration among the Eight Schools, that convenes an annual meeting and sponsors online course development.

Today schools are offering their students real world opportunities for entrepreneurship and innovation. Following Harvard's Innovation Lab (i-lab) model, schools such as Lawrenceville, Deerfield, and Choate Rosemary Hall, are promoting design thinking, applied science and math, reverse engineering, hands-on experimentation, three-dimensional prototyping (mock-ups), and a more flexible course of study to encourage collaboration and cross-disciplinary projects.

THE WHOLE STUDENT: TEACHING AND LEARNING

Northfield Mount Herman School Rhodes Center for the Arts

VISUAL AND PERFORMING ARTS SPACES

Academic courses in the visual and performing arts are the most recent erosion of the traditional classical curriculum. While students had performed plays, music, and dance—often with faculty direction—these endeavors remained part of the extra-curriculum until the 1960s. Art history was considered worthy of academic credit, but creating art was not; reading Shakespeare's plays was an essential part of the curriculum, performing them was not; music "appreciation" was curricular, a piano recital was not.

Yale University led the way in elevating the arts to curricular status, not only for college preparatory schools, but for other colleges and universities. The Trumbull Gallery—built as a freestanding building on the old campus in 1832—was the earliest introduction of visual art in an academic context. Yale established an art school in 1864, a music department in 1889, an art museum in 1908, an architecture school in 1916, and a drama department in 1924. For students to nurture their artistic talents, but not for academic credit, there are many legendary performing groups at Ivy League universities. Among them are the Yale's Whiffenpoofs, Penn's Mask and Wig, Princeton's Triangle, and Harvard's Hasty Pudding.

Students also drove the arts at the early academies and later college preparatory schools. At Choate, for example, students started an orchestra in 1908, a glee club in 1911, and a musical theater club in the 1930s. They often preformed Gilbert and Sullivan operettas with boys playing the female roles. However, with a gift from Paul Mellon—son of Andrew Mellon who had previously funded the library and a science building—the school opened a performing arts center in 1972. Students were then required to take arts

The Lawrenceville School Guss Center for the Visual Arts

courses for credit. The building, designed by the eminent architect I. M. Pei,[23] includes a 799 seat theater and an experimental, "black box" theater in one wing, and in another wing, art studios, an art gallery, and rehearsal and practice studios for music and dance students. Pei's decision to split the building in two wings to create a through passage between them is symbolic. At the time, Rosemary Hall, a girl's school in Greenwich, Connecticut, merged with Choate and moved to Wallingford. The gateway connects the former all boys school campus with new buildings for Rosemary Hall. Like Choate Rosemary Hall, Northfield Mount Hermon constructed an arts center when the two campuses were consolidated in 2005. The Rhodes Center for the Arts, designed by Childs, Bertman, Tseckares, includes practice and performance spaces for theater, dance, and music, as well as studio and exhibition space for the visual arts. The building occupies a site where Mount Hermon's original academic buildings—Recitation Hall (1885) and Silliman Laboratory (1892), both destroyed by fire—were located. Viewed from Grass Hill on the west, the building appears modest, but because the site slopes dramatically to the east, most of the building's visual interest is on the downslope side. Shed roofs, board and batten siding, and linear clerestory windows, give the impression of barns and nineteenth-century industrial buildings of the Connecticut River valley.

Other members of the Eight Schools Association, introduced arts into the curriculum in the 1960s and 1970s. Lawrenceville, for example, developed an arts district with three separate buildings rather than one large building to house all arts venues. To encourage public attendance at performances and exhibitions, the school provides a convenient entrance from Route 206 (Main Street) and public parking. The first, the

THE WHOLE STUDENT: TEACHING AND LEARNING

Phillips Academy
Andover
Elson Center (left)
Addison Gallery
of American Art (right)

Hotchkiss School
Eastman Music Center

Kirby Arts Center, opened in 1963 for the Department of Performing Arts. The building was designed to harmonize with the pre-World War II campus, but also acknowledges influences of modern architecture. The main entrance features a pediment supported by four columns and entablature, but the columns and pediment are unadorned. The exterior walls are red brick, but are detailed with sharp corners and punched openings. The roof is sloped and finished with slate tiles, but there are no dormers, cupolas, or chimneys. There is a wood cornice at the transition of the roof and walls, but its profile is flat, not carved.

The two other buildings in the arts district are the Gruss Center for the Visual Arts and the Juliet Lyell Staunton Clark Music Center, built in 2000. The Gruss Center comprises a renovation of the school's first library—designed in 1931 by Delano & Aldrich[24] in a Colonial Revival Style—and an addition designed by Graham Gund in a compatible but contemporary style in 1998. The addition features a barrel vaulted, standing seam, metal roof that references the hemispherical dome over the porticoed entry to the former library and the segmented domed roof. The Clark Music Center's exterior window walls and floating roofline are bold statements visible across an expansive lawn to passersby on Route 206. A pair of full height arched window openings enlivened with a grid of horizontal and vertical mullions that recall Frank Lloyd Wright's compositions, provides daylight and backdrop for flat floor performance spaces.

Notable buildings for the arts at other Eight Schools campuses include the Addison Gallery of American Art at Andover, designed by Charles A. Platt in 1931, and the Esther Eastman Music Center at Hotchkiss, designed by Centerbrook Architects in 2005. Platt was in the midst of re-visioning the entire Andover campus when the school's largest benefactor, Thomas Cochran, provided funds for the gallery building, an endowment, and its core collection. The Elson Art Center for studio art, added to the gallery in 1963, connects the making and studying of art. This connection was considered, but rejected, at the time Platt was designing the gallery.[25] The Eastman Center at Hotchkiss is the most recent in a long sequence of additions over one hundred years to the Main Building. The four-story building occupies a most desirable site overlooking Lake Wononscopomuc. It is integrated with the Main's continuous corridor and the 1966 Walker Auditorium.

SUMMARY

Teaching and learning are critical components of a school's mission to educate the whole student. Both curricula and pedagogy evolved over time: classical to liberal; religious to secular; recitation to discussion and research; required courses to electives and independent study; and capstone courses to advanced placement. New building types and teaching spaces evolved to support the curriculum and pedagogy. Grades matter, but in today's competitive college admission environment, perhaps the greatest advantage—and most distinctive characteristic—of a boarding school is its residential character. The next chapter, boarding and bonding, explores this aspect of the whole student.

Notes

1 - St. Paul's did not follow this course. "Unlike the academies such as Andover, Deerfield, and Exeter, or later the 'feeder schools' like Lawrenceville and Hotchkiss, St. Paul's did not care to adjust itself to the entrance requirements of other institutions." *A Brief History of St. Paul's School*, pages 15–16.

2 - *After the Harkness gift: a history of Phillips Exeter Academy since 1930*, page 24.

3 - ibid. page 28.

4 - ibid. pages 90–92.

5 - Other participating schools are Loomis Chaffee School, Milton Academy, Miss Porter's School, and Taft School.

6 - Edward S. Harkness (1874–1940) a graduate of St. Paul's Schools and Yale University, managed his family's foundation that supported medical research and education. Between 1920 and 1930 he donated over 6.5 million dollars to Phillips Exeter Academy.

7 - Lewis Perry (1877–1970) was headmaster of Phillips Exeter Academy (his alma mater) from 1914 to 1946. Prior to his appointment as Exeter's eighth headmaster, he taught English at Williams College (also his alma mater). During his tenure, Perry shepherded Edward Harkness' gifts and implemented his educational concepts.

8 - Ralph Adams Cram (active 1890s to 1930s) was principal in the Boston firm of Cram and Ferguson. The firm designed eighteen buildings for Phillips Exeter Academy, and for other prep schools including Choate and St. Paul's. Cram's designs for the Graduate College and University Chapel for Princeton are the epitome of the Collegiate Gothic style.

9 - *After the Harkness gift: a history of Phillips Exeter Academy since 1930*, page 206.

10 - *Benjamin Franklin: in search of a better world*, page 103.

11 - Ernest Flagg (active 1890s to 1930s) attended the École des-Beaux Arts from 1888–1892 and translated the style known as Academic Classicism to America. He maintained an office in New York City where he designed residential and commercial buildings, he Corcoran Gallery of Art in Washington, D.C., and the United States Naval Academy in Annapolis, Maryland. His connection with St. Paul's School and the Sheldon family was likely facilitated by his family relation to the Scribner family.

12 - The building is currently used as the admission office.

13 - Robert A. M. Stern FAIA (active 1960s to the present) is principal of his eponymous firm and former professor and dean of the Yale School of Architecture. His firm, known for its stylistic preference for post-modernism, designed innumerable buildings for prep schools, colleges and universities, including four of the Eight Schools and six Ivy League universities.

14 - *Architectural Record* August 1991, pages 58–62

15 - Louis I. Kahn (active 1930s to 1970s) was a Philadelphia based architect and professor of architecture at the University of Pennsylvania and Yale University schools of architecture. He is well known for his singular style of monumental modernism as expressed in museums, research laboratories, government buildings and private residences.

16 - Graham Gund (active 1970s to the present) is president of the Gund Partnership located in Cambridge, MA. Over the past forty-plus years, his firm has deigned many arts, cultural, and learning environments in the northeast and midwest, particularly for New England prep schools such as Taft, Groton, and Westminster and colleges such as Mount Holyoke.

17 - *The American College and University*, pages 228–233.

18 - *Deerfield 1797–1997: a pictorial history of the academy*, page 39.

19 - ibid. pages 65 and 78.

20 - Charles A. Platt (active 1900s to 1930s) maintained an architectural practice in New York City, and membership in an art colony in Cornish, New Hampshire. His stylistic preference was for Colonial Revival and Italian Renaissance. He designed buildings for Andover, Deerfield, and Northfield as well as art museums, and landscapes for estates of

prominent families.

21 - Skidmore Owings and Merrill (active 1950s to the present) is one of the largest architectural and engineering firms in the United States with projects and offices around the world. David Childs, a principal in the firm and graduate of Deerfield Academy, designed Deerfield's science laboratory and natatorium.

22 - Cesar Pelli (active 1960s to the present) is a principal of Pelli Clarke Pelli in New Haven, Connecticut. In his early career, he worked for Eero Saarinen and later became dean of the Yale University School of Architecture. Among the firm's projects for education are buildings for Yale University, Vassar College, and Princeton University.

23 - Ioeh Ming Pei (active 1950s to 1990s) founded his eponymous firm in 1955 and was principal of Pei Cobb Freed, the successor firm, until his retirement from practice in 1990. Pei was chair of the Department of Architecture at the Harvard Graduate School of Design. Cobb is a graduate of Phillips Exeter Academy. In addition to science and arts buildings at Choate Rosemary Hall, the firms designed buildings for Harvard, Cornell, and Princeton.

24 - Delano & Aldrich (active 1900s to 1930s). William Delano was a graduate of The Lawrenceville School and the École des Beaux-Arts. Both Delano and Aldrich worked for Carrere and Hastings in New York before starting their own firm. Their stylistic preference was for Academic Classicism and Georgian Revival. The firm, and its successor firm Campbell Aldrich and Nutly, designed buildings for Hotchkiss, Northfield, Mount Hermon, and Lawrenceville, as well as for Yale and Cornell.

25 - *The Campus Guide: Phillips Academy Andover*, pages 136–38.

Choate Rosemary Hall
Memorial House

3: THE WHOLE STUDENT: BOARDING AND BONDING

We become responsible for their manners, habits, and morals, no less than their progress in useful knowledge…"

1823 Prospectus of the Round Hill School

This excerpt from the Round Hill prospectus distills the essence of a boarding school education. In the early years of academies such as Andover, Exeter, Deerfield, and Lawrenceville, however, most students lived with their families in town or in the surrounding countryside. Students from more distant parts of the country took room and board with local families, or in private boarding houses. The academies licensed these facilities and issued regulations, but, in reality, had diminished opportunity to form the "manners, habits, and morals" of their students.[1] The academies did provide rudimentary on-campus housing for "charity" students, whose families could not afford private boarding houses.

The founders of the Round Hill School in Northampton, Massachusetts, were focused on creating a "family boarding academy." George Bancroft and Joseph Cogswell—both graduates of Exeter and Harvard—had visited progressive schools in Switzerland, Germany (Prussia), and England before founding Round Hill in 1823. On their travels they developed ideas about an enlightened curriculum and the "whole student" character of the ideal boarding school.[2] Although the school closed in 1834, it became a model for later boarding schools such as St. Paul's School.[3] Founded in 1858 in Concord, New Hampshire, by George Shattuck[4]—himself an alumnus of Round Hill—St. Paul's has always been an on-campus boarding school. Until the school built its first dormitory in 1869, students at St. Paul's lived and studied in Shattuck's summer home, called "the mother house." The Reverend Dwight Moody[5] founded the Northfield Seminary for Young Ladies in 1879, and the Mount Hermon School for Boys in 1881, on this same model.

Existing academies began constructing on-campus housing for students in earnest in the late 1800s. They followed the lead of schools like Round Hill and St. Paul's, but also emulated the colleges for whom their students were preparing.[6] Exeter built its first dormitory, Abbott Hall, in 1855 and finally discontinued use of private boarding houses in 1942.[7] Schools founded in the early 1900s, such as Choate and Hotchkiss, avoided rooming and boarding houses altogether. Today all Eight Schools—except St. Paul's—enroll day students, from nearby communities who prefer to live at home. The goal of on-campus housing is to help bond students to each other, students to faculty, and students to the school. In the process, the schools hope to curb bad behavior, protect students from harmful outside influences, and ultimately foster devoted alumni. This ideal of a family boarding academy, however, is compromised when "bonding" becomes inappropriately intimate.

The following sections explore student housing, dining halls, and social centers, which

St. Paul's School
Shattuck Summer Home

together contribute to "student life." Faculty housing—on campus and in surrounding neighborhoods—enhances community building. Specific building types have evolved to serve these needs.

STUDENT HOUSING

Once academies and newly-founded boarding schools embraced the goal of housing all out-of-town students on campus, they experimented with several arrangements. The cottage plan is an attempt to recreate the family home, with a faculty master as paterfamilias. Another type is the multi-story dormitory with private rooms, shared bathrooms, and common rooms, supervised by a live-in bachelor teacher, or in the case of an all-girls school, a non-faculty housemother. Still another type is a dormitory with an attached wing for a faculty member, oftentimes married with children. Schools often provide shared dormitory rooms for day students while they are on campus.

COTTAGE PLAN

Lawrenceville Academy, originally known as Maidenhead Academy, was founded by the local Presbyterian minister Isaac Van Arsdale Brown in 1810. The campus consisted of Brown's house and a classroom building. Like its contemporaries, the school only provided housing for charity students. Accommodations were minimal, consisting of a ward, or barracks, with a curtain separating one bunk from another. An outhouse and cold water bathhouse were the only sanitary facilities. Local students lived at home, and others lived with host families or in private boarding houses. The third proprietor, Dr. Samuel Hamill, changed the school's name to the Classical and Commercial High School, to reflect an expanded curriculum, but made no attempt update the living arrangements.

In 1883, the estate of John Cleve Green, an early alumnus, purchased the high school from Hamill and transformed it into a college preparatory boarding school.[8] Green had attended the College of New Jersey in Princeton, five miles along the main road from Lawrenceville. He earned a fortune that enabled him to fund capital projects and academic initiatives at the college. When James McCosh, the college president, expressed the need for better-qualified applicants, Green and the trustees of his estate provided an endowment, purchased additional land, and built new facilities for a revived Lawrenceville School.

One of the trustees' first initiatives, in addition to hiring James MacKenzie as headmaster, was to hire Frederick Law Olmsted[9] to plan an enlarged campus, and Peabody & Stearns[10] to design the buildings. Frederick Olmsted and Robert Peabody were neighbors in Brookline, the planned garden suburb of Boston.[11] They applied this model to their design for the expanded Lawrenceville campus. Olmsted laid out a broad

The Lawrenceville School
Kennedy House

circle, bordered by buildings, that enclosed a lawn populated with trees. Peabody designed five cottages at the perimeter of one third of the circle, a chapel at the midpoint, and an academic building and upper-class dorm on the opposing third.[12]

The cottages, initially called masters houses, each held about twenty boys and a faculty master on three floors. The first floor, slightly elevated from the ground, contained a dining room and kitchen, a "lounging room," the house master's study, and student rooms. There were two types of student accommodations: one a single room and the other a suite containing two bedrooms with a common study. The upper floors contained servants' quarters, the master's chambers, and a mix of student rooms. While the houses had indoor plumbing, a common bath house provided the only bathing facilities. Designed in a modified Queen Anne style, the cottages resembled grand houses found in Brookline. The exterior—while somewhat varied from building to building—followed an irregular interior plan, providing projections and recesses for a round tower, roofed porches, and a composition of intersecting steep rooflines with gable ends. Departing from Queen Anne residential precedents, Peabody used brick, in lieu of wood clapboard, for walls, and slate, in lieu of wood shingles, for roofing. These materials expressed durability and permanence, and relate to the heavier stone masonry of the other buildings on the circle. One hundred years later, in preparation for the arrival of female students, the school constructed five additional cottages on a curvilinear spur connected to the circle. Designed by Short and Ford, these cottages are a post-modern interpretation of the Peabody design. The Olmsted circle and the Peabody buildings, all constructed from 1884 to 1895, are on the National Register of Historic Places.[13]

Mount Hermon School for Boys—founded in 1881 by Reverend Dwight Moody near Gill, Massachusetts—built a row of five

The Lawrenceville School
McClellen House

Northfield Mount
Hermon School
Cottage Row

cottages for its inaugural class. The middle cottage served as the kitchen for the four residential cottages. All are located on Grass Ridge with eastward views of the Connecticut River valley and mountains beyond. Designed by Eugene C. Gardner in the Queen Anne style, the buildings feature red brick and wood shingle walls, granite foundation walls and window trim, steep slate roofs, and decorative woodwork.[14] To accommodate an influx of students, the school built two large conventional dormitories and a dining hall between 1898 and 1915. To prepare for the arrival of girls on campus in 2005, Sasaski Associates designed additional cottages in line with, and stylistically related to, the nineteenth–century ones.

EIGHT SCHOOLS CAMPUS AND CULTURE

Hotchkiss School
Tinker (Alumni)

Hotchkiss School
Bissell Commons

DORMITORY MODEL

The Hotchkiss School, founded in 1891 in Lakeville, Connecticut, adopted the dormitory model from the beginning. When Hotchkiss commissioned Cass Gilbert[15] in 1915 to prepare a master plan for long-range growth, the campus consisted of one dormitory and a school building known simply as Main. Gilbert planned two open courtyards defined by three dormitories symmetrically placed on either side of a wide axial mall leading to Main. Each of the dormitories originally provided rooms for approximately 60 boys and four faculty on four floors. The ground floor includes a reception hall and bedrooms. The upper floors include student rooms and bachelor

Deerfield Academy
Dining Hall

masters' rooms, served by a double-loaded (central) corridor and common bathrooms. Between 1923 and 1928, two Gilbert-designed dormitories and an infirmary—later converted to a dormitory—were built. These buildings established not only the parameters of the master plan, but the defining Georgian Revival architectural style of the campus.

Gilbert's version of Georgian Revival features a rectangular plan, exterior red brick walls, symmetrically placed windows with stone headers and sills, and a central entry elaborated by a Greek inspired wood portico. He separated the sloping slate roof—with dormers for the fourth floor rooms—from the brick walls with a projected cornice. The segmented roofline and two end elevations distinguish Gilbert's design from other similar building types. Where one would expect a ridge, he terminated the sloping roof segments with a flat portion framed by a wood balustrade. Where one would expect a gable end, he designed paired chimneys rising above the roofline, joined by a parapet concealing the flat roof.

After Gilbert resigned in 1929 following a dispute over challenges to his master plan, the New York firm Delano and Aldrich designed the next generation of dormitories. Between 1931 and 1936, the firm designed two dormitories following, in general, Gilbert's campus plan and architectural style. The buildings are three stories in an L-shaped plan with married faculty apartments in the projecting end wing. Departures from Gilbert's design include bracketing the windows with shutters, brick quoins at the corners, and a pedimented entry. Between 2007 and 2016, Robert Stern's firm RAMSA designed three additional dormitories, forming a courtyard northeast of Main. Gilbert's plan a century earlier, anticipated expansion in this direction. The most recent building is a replacement for Bissell Hall, the original dormitory named after the school's founder. Stern's design follows both Gilbert's and

Phillips Academy
Andover
Dining Commons

Delano and Aldrich's precedents, but with greater elaboration in plan and detail.

DINING HALLS

Eating a meal together provides an opportunity for socialization, making friends, and imbibing the culture. Before academies began providing room and board, students ate meals with their own family, with a host family, or in a private boarding house.[16] The transition to on-campus housing afforded the opportunity for students to bond through shared dining. The cottage type housing as described above, includes a dining room and kitchen. Paid staff prepared and served meals to the house master and the resident students. At times, if the master were married, his wife might perform these duties. In contemporary cooperative households, students themselves might shop for, or even grow, their own food, prepare and serve it, and clean up. Before refrigeration, supermarkets, and food service companies, many schools owned farms that produced vegetables, fruit, dairy products, and sometimes meat for the campus community.

As more students lived on campus, and the number of students exceeded the ability to provide meals economically to small groups, schools provided dining halls with commercial kitchens. These spaces were located in either a freestanding building, or appended to a dormitory or dormitory quadrangle. Before the 1970s, dining halls reflected the hierarchical nature of the schools. Meals were served on a fixed schedule, with a predetermined menu. Assigned seating at, in most cases, rectangular tables placed the older students toward the head of the table and the younger ones toward the lower end. A faculty member would usually sit at the head to model behavior and stimulate discussion. At the evening meal, some combination of the headmaster, distinguished guests, senior faculty, and class

THE WHOLE STUDENT: BOARDING AND BONDING

Phillips Exeter Academy
Phelps Academy Center

Choate Rosemary Hall
St. John Center

representatives would sit at a head table. A dress code—jackets and ties for boys—was enforced, and attendance was mandatory. After the social upheavals of the 1960s–70s, these arrangements were replaced with broadly scheduled meal times, self-service menu choices, round tables with open seating, and a relaxed dress code. A private dining room is usually available for more formal occasions. Deerfield Academy, however, offers five sit-down dinners a week, with dress code and shared waiter service.

Commons, as the dining hall at Andover is known, was built in 1929 on the site of an eighteenth-century tavern. The building is located close to the center of campus in a quadrangle defined by two dormitories and two academic buildings. It is the first dining hall built to serve the entire academy community. In the nineteenth century, students living on campus formed their own "eating clubs" or, if living in town, had meals at their boarding houses. In 1902, to engage more students with the campus culture, the school renovated one of the older academic buildings for use as a dining hall. "The Beanery," as students nicknamed the dining hall, served this function until Commons was completed. Originally, the building contained four dining rooms, one for each class. Marble portals, wood-paneled walls, and chandeliers afforded elegant dining. A 2009 renovation that followed a cafeteria-food court model, modernized food service. One of the dining rooms was converted into a cafe and an outdoor terrace, accessible from the lower level student lounge, was added.[17]

STUDENT CENTERS

In the 1960s, as the student population became more diverse—and as the era of privilege and exclusion receded—the need for a common meeting place grew in importance. Creation of student centers to meet this need represents the capstone of a school's mission to develop the whole student. While dormitories, classrooms, dining halls, gymnasiums, playing fields, and chapels each address specific aspects of student life, a student center can fill the gaps and bring the community together. The University of Pennsylvania pioneered the student union movement in the late nineteenth century and Harvard followed suit in 1901.[18] Other colleges and secondary schools gradually moved in this direction, consolidating various informal gathering and organized extracurricular activities found in scattered campus locations. Some students preferred off-campus, privately run stores like the Jigger Shop in Lawrenceville. Made popular by Owen Johnson's *The Varmint*—a fictionalized account of student life at The Lawrenceville School in the early twentieth century—the shop provided students a place to hang out between recitations, while serving ice cream sundaes in a soda fountain glass known as a jigger. After the shop burned in 1990, it was reincarnated as the student store in the main campus dining hall.

The Phelps Academy Center that opened at Exeter in 2006 illustrates the evolution of the student center building type.[19] Almost ninety years earlier, the editors of the school newspaper had argued for a student union that would become "the social center of the school, elevate school spirit, improve morals and morale, and promote equality and democracy."[20] When the science department moved to a new building in 2001, it afforded the opportunity to consolidate dispersed and disparate facilities in a thoroughly renovated, centrally located building.[21] The building is located in a quadrangle, defined by two academic buildings and the central administration building. Together with an abutting dormitory and dining quadrangle, this mixed-use zone ensures that the center will be populated around the clock. The quadrangle's open lawn may be used for large outdoor gatherings, often sheltered by a tent. Diagonal pathways entering, crossing, and leaving the quadrangle attest to the notion that the building occupies a crossroads of the campus, both symbolically and literally.

The original three-story science building, with two-story wings added later, was designed by Ralph Adams Cram. The repurposed spaces include a main floor lounge, a grill/cafe, post office and mailboxes, a 200-seat multi-purpose auditorium, offices for the student newspaper and student activities, the student radio station, music practice rooms, and an art studio, as well as a day student suite. The suite functions as a home away from home for day students, and contains

Deerfield Academy
The Manse

active and quiet lounges, lockers, showers, and meeting space.

Among the other Eight Schools, Choate Rosemary Hall opened a purpose-built student center building in 2017. It is attached to the original, prominent dormitory building that has since grown to include the main dining hall, classrooms, and faculty offices. Lawrenceville's current strategic plan envisions a community-wide social and dining space.

FACULTY HOUSING

The ability of students and faculty to interact outside the classroom contributes to a school's boarding and bonding mission. A school may provide on-campus, or near-campus, housing for faculty to help accomplish this goal, but there is another important motivation. As part of a compensation package, subsidized housing is a powerful recruiting and retention device. Junior and unmarried faculty may be provided rooms in student dormitories, along with a duty to supervise, but also befriend, students. Married faculty are often housed in an apartment attached to a dormitory. Senior faculty may be provided single-family homes on the campus periphery. These permanent residents serve to represent the school in the community and to promote good will, but also to advocate for the school's interests. The head of school usually lives on campus in a private home, symbolic of accessibility, but also of authority and continuity. Students come and go every four years, but the senior faculty and administration tend to stay for decades.

Some Deerfield Academy faculty and the head of school live in restored eighteenth-century and early nineteenth-century houses on the town's Main Street. The histories of the town of Deerfield and Deerfield Academy are intertwined. In the 1940s, Helen and Henry Flynt—whose son was in the class of 1936 at the academy—settled in Deerfield and, over time, purchased and ren-

Phillips Academy Andover
Churchill House

ovated twelve houses. Several are now open to the public as house museums operated by Historic Deerfield, and others were purchased by the academy for use as faculty apartments.[22] The academy also constructed three houses on Main Street—designed with similar characteristics of neighboring private houses from past centuries—to provide housing for faculty and rooms for students.

"Faculty Row," on the west side of Main Street in Andover, is similar to the row of historic houses on Deerfield's Main Street. The Andover Theological Seminary had custom-built five houses between 1810 and 1835 as means to recruit eminent theologians. When the seminary moved in 1909, Phillips Academy bought the houses for its faculty.[23] Between 1880 and 1920, the academy built and acquired additional houses on Main Street. One of the largest burned in 1887, and another was moved in the 1920s to open a vista toward the mountains on axis with the main school building across the street. In the 1930s, Perry Shaw & Hepburn—the firm that designed Colonial Williamsburg—designed five additional faculty houses in their signature style, on a cul-de-sac connected to Main Street.

SUMMARY

To a large extent, a student's "manners, habits, and morals" are formed by the bonding enabled by buildings designed for living, dining, and socializing. The next two chapters, one on diversity and inclusion, and the other on athletics and spirituality, explore additional means to form the whole student.

THE WHOLE STUDENT: BOARDING AND BONDING

Notes

1 - *American Boarding Schools: a historical study*, page 104.

2 - Johann Pestalozzi—known as the "father of modern education"— advocated schooling that cultivated the "head, heart, and hands" of his students. His research is the foundation of progressive thought in the development of the whole child/student: intellectual, moral, and physical.

3 - *American Boarding Schools: a historical study*, page 136.

4 - George Cheyne Shattuck, Jr., (1813–1893) like his father, was a physician practicing in Boston in the early-to-mid-eighteen-hundreds. He was educated at Boston Latin School, The Round Hill Academy, and Harvard College. He was a professor of medicine at the Harvard Medical School from 1855 to 1873. He married into an Episcopalian family and became an evangelist for the faith. His schooling, teaching, and religion led him to found St. Paul's School.

5 - Dwight Lyman Moody (1837–1899) grew up in Northfield, Massachusetts, in a single-parent family. At age nineteen Moody moved to Chicago where he became a successful businessman and evangelical preacher. He founded the Moody Bible Institute that generated revenue by publishing hymnals. With his wealth and belief in Christian education as a means of evangelism, he founded the Northfield Seminary for Young Ladies near his family's homestead in 1879. Two years later he founded Mount Hermon School for boys several miles south of Northfield.

6 - Harvard, Princeton, and Yale started building large-scale dormitories in the 1870s. Yale had demolished smaller eighteenth- and nineteenth-century dormitories.

7 - *After the Harkness Gift: a history of Phillips Exeter Academy since 1930*, page 116.

8 - *A Circle in Time: Frederick Law Olmsted's design for the Lawrenceville School*, page 49.

9 - Frederick Law Olmsted (active 1860s–1900s) is considered the first American landscape architect. He combined his experiential understanding of nature with an education in civil engineering. He was superintendent of the construction of Central Park in New York City that led to a partnership with Calvert Vaux, the designer of the park. Together they designed urban parks in Brooklyn, Buffalo, Chicago, Boston, and other cities. Olmsted formed a partnership with his brother and later two of his sons. They expanded their services to town planning, suburban subdivisions, conservation, and most importantly for this book, campus planning.

10 - Peabody & Stearns, see note 23 Chapter One.

11 - *Community By Design: The Olmsted firm and the development of Brookline, Massachusetts*, pages 67–69.

12 - *A Circle in Time: Frederick Law Olmsted's design for the Lawrenceville School*, pages 65–69.

13 - National Park Service, 1985.

14 - *Lift Thine Eyes: the landscape, the buildings, the heritage of Northfield Mount Hermon School*, pages 74–76.

15 - Cass Gilbert (active 1880s–1930s), whose offices were located first in St. Paul Minnesota and later New York City, designed museums, libraries, state capitols, and most famously the Woolworth Building skyscraper in 1913. His campus plan for the University of Minnesota completed in 1910 was likely a factor in his commissions for Hotchkiss.

16 - Boarding school and boarding houses are misnomers. Board refers to meals. Today's boarding schools provide both room and board.

17 - Paresky Commons and its Heritage, andover.edu/student life, accessed June 2017.

18 - Houston Hall—the student center at the University of Pennsylvania—opened in 1895. The Harvard Union opened in 1901.

19 - *After the Harkness Gift: a history of Phillips Exeter Academy since 1930*, page 147.

20 - *Phillips Exeter Academy Bulletin* April 1919.

21 - Princeton University's campus center opened in 2000. The building's original occupant was, like Exeter, the Physics Department.

22 -   *Deerfield 1797–1997: a pictorial history of the academy,* page 130.

23 -   *The Campus Guide: Phillips Academy Andover,* pages 46, 47.

The Deerfield Boy   The Deerfield Girl

4: THE WHOLE STUDENT: DIVERSITY AND INCLUSION

True diversity demands inclusion—not just having a seat at the table but also having an equal voice in the conversation.
        Cecelia Rouse, dean of the Woodrow Wilson School, Princeton University[1]

Education derives primarily not from schools and colleges but from a diversity of experience. Two sexes are twice as diverse as one.
        Headmaster Seymour St. John, Choate School c. 1968[2]

Until the 1950s, a student at a private college preparatory boarding school (prep school) would likely be a WASP—a white anglo-saxon protestant. Add to that characterization, male and affluent. Liberation era consciousness raising, peer pressure, and enrollment declines drove private schools to open their admissions to a more diverse pool of applicants, including females, people of color, socio-economic groups, and faith traditions that disrupted the WASP profile.[3]

After World War II, schools realized that to encourage qualified students from underprivileged families to apply for admission they would have to reach out and to provide scholarships. In 1945, Exeter, for example, named a Director of Scholarship Boys whose job it was to visit Boy Scout troops, Rotary Clubs, and other community organizations in an attempt to counter the perception that private boarding schools were only for the privileged. The next year, the school launched a campaign to fund an endowment for increased scholarship aid. Once scholarship boys were enrolled, unlike boys from wealthier families, they were required to hold jobs, such as waiting on faculty tables.[4] This practice, not uncommon for prep schools at the time, has since been discontinued. Today, all Eight Schools reach out to non-traditional students worldwide and have endowments to provide financial aid.

Civil rights and equal opportunity were the hallmarks of the 1960s nationwide. In 1963, the not-for-profit A Better Chance (ABC) was founded to "increase substantially the number of well-educated young people of color who are capable of assuming positions of responsibility and leadership in American society."[5] To implement this mission, ABC provided scholarships for deserving middle school students to participate in summer programs at private schools. Members of the Eight Schools Association (ESA) were more than willing to offer these programs to further their diversity goals and agreed to admit students who successfully completed the program.[6] Once admitted, however, some students of color found it difficult to adjust to an unfamiliar and sometimes hostile environment. The schools provided counseling services to promote better understanding of racial issues, but the challenge was to balance assimilation with identity. Black students formed African American centers and argued for hiring more teachers of color and introducing multicultural courses in the curriculum.[7]

Religious diversity also challenged the predominant WASP culture in the 1960s. In their formative years, members of the ESA built chapels and required students to attend daily worship services. Theology and bible study classes were integral to the curriculum. These services and courses reflected the Protestant beliefs of the founders and subsequent leaders, many of whom were clergymen. This bias alienated the few Roman Catholic and Jewish students who, as their numbers increased, started identity-based clubs and argued for a more inclusive curriculum and faculty. One outcome of the liberation era disruption was the relaxation of mandatory chapel attendance.[8]

All Eight Schools were open only to male students well into the twentieth century.[9] The decision to admit female students to all-male schools, and males to all-female schools, was perhaps the most disruptive in the movement toward inclusion. It affected students, faculty, staff, and the facilities that support them. All-female private schools, beginning with Emma Willard School in 1814, offered a secondary school education for girls, but there were no women's colleges for graduates to attend until Vassar was founded in 1865.[10] Except for Oberlin College, founded in 1833 in Ohio, there were no coeducational private colleges in the U.S. until the 1860s. As a result, some private girls' schools offered college-level courses. One such course, moral philosophy, was considered the capstone of a college education, and was often taught by the president.[11] Other private girls' schools with lesser academic objectives gained a reputation as finishing schools. Boys were "fit" for college, and girls were "finished" for polite society.

Beginning in the late 1960s, boarding school enrollment declined precipitously as public high schools and private day schools graduated students, female and male, with superior academic credentials, athletic prowess, and arts proficiency.[12] The "best boys" from the secondary school applicant pool increasingly chose to attend coeducational colleges. All male colleges, and by extension all male boarding schools, began moving toward coeducation, but not without controversy. In her 2016 book *Keep the Damned Women Out,* Nancy Weiss Malkiel, Princeton University's former dean of the college, elucidates the basic questions the trustees considered in 1969: will Princeton be good for women? Will women be good for Princeton? The answer: the university admitted its first class of women in 1970.

For prep schools, the questions went deeper. Since their students were minors, the schools were legally "in loco parentis."[13] Sexual misconduct was perhaps the most troubling behavior that school administrators and trustees faced. During the all-male era, relations between two male students, or between a male faculty member and male student, were in some cases suppressed, only to surface many years later. When considering admission of girls, the questions became even more troubling. While the possibility of relations between a boy and a girl student or between a faculty member and a girl student were a concern, schools were slow to develop policies relating to sexual harassment, misconduct, and abuse. Gone were the days when a headmaster could quote a student saying "we don't have any rules, but if you break one, you get it in the neck."[14] Today, when transgressions surface, schools opt for transparency and concern for the victim rather than suppression and concern for the school's reputation.[15] To help students cope with sexual issues—as well as drug and alcohol abuse, bullying, and other social disorders—schools created counseling centers.

The first woman to lead one of the ESA schools was Kendra O'Donnell (1987–1997) at

Choate Rosemary Hall
Squire Stanley

Exeter, who made diversity her top priority.[16] Since then, five of the eight schools have had a woman as head of school. Gradually, as the ranks of female graduates increased, women assumed leadership positions in the alumni association and the board of trustees. Niche, a for-profit, on-line company that ranks public and private schools nationwide, publishes an annual report titled "Most Diverse Private High Schools in America" that measures racial, cultural, and gender diversity.[17] For 2017, six ESA members ranked in the top twelve percent.

    The following sections examine the way some of the Eight Schools addressed coeducation: merging with an existing girls' school; establishing an affiliated girls' school; and gradual admission of girls. By 1989, all eight were engaged in some form of coeducation.

CHOATE AND ROSEMARY HALL MERGER

Mary Atwater Choate was a fifth generation member of a family that owned farmland in rural Wallingford, Connecticut. In 1890, she opened a girls boarding school, Rosemary Hall, in the farm's main house and hired a young British woman, Caroline Ruutz-Rees,[18] as headmistress. Six years later, Mary Atwater's husband William G. Choate, a successful lawyer and judge in New York City, opened a boys' boarding school on the property, but with a separate schoolhouse and faculty. The building, known as Squire Stanley for its eighteenth-century owner, was constructed in 1690 and expanded in 1770. It still serves as a dormitory.

    It was not long before Ms. Ruutz-Rees' aspiration for a truly academic school clashed with Mrs. Choate's notion of a finishing school. In 1900, Ruutz-Rees accepted an offer of land and funds from parents of current students to move the school to Greenwich, Connecticut. Theodore Blake, an architect whose portfolio included par-

Rosemary Hall
Campus Plan

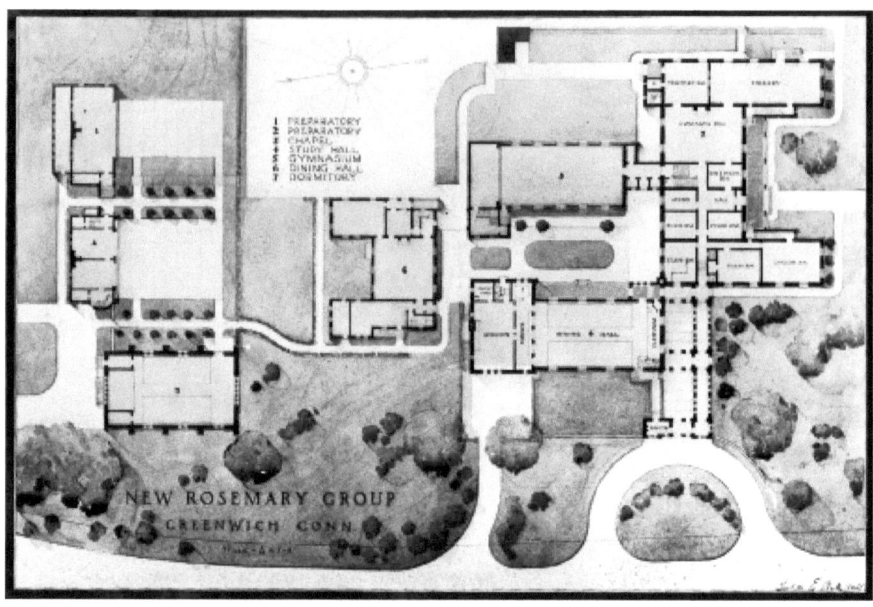

ish churches and country estates, planned most of the early campus. For Ruutz-Rees, "the school was her showpiece. Everything about it bore the markings of her style. She loved things Italian."[19] In ecclesiastical matters, however, her preference was for English Gothic. Blake designed the chapel—named Saint Bede's by Ruutz-Rees in honor of the patron saint of education—to appear as if it were transported intact from the English countryside. The school attracted gifted, well-bred students and was regarded as one of the top girls' prep schools in the east. In 1948, however, the school faced a financial crisis. The school was overly dependent on tuition revenue as it had almost no endowment. Even with low faculty salaries, the school ran an annual budget deficit and was in debt for a loan taken to rebuild the main hall that had been destroyed by fire. By 1936, enrollment had dropped from a high of 200 students to ninety-one students.[20]

Back in Wallingford, George St. John was appointed headmaster of the fledging boys' school in 1908. Upon his arrival, he observed "there was little that spelled permanence or bespoke a school."[21] During his forty-year tenure, he developed a complete campus by erecting eight academic and residential buildings and moving and renovating more than twenty existing houses. Hill House, a multi-purpose residential, dining, and academic building, was the first. It is sited on a ridge that overlooks the campus and set the Georgian Revival style for future buildings. After World War I, to honor the fifteen Choate boys who died in military service, Memorial House dormitory was built on the same ridge. Next was a chapel, and later an infirmary, both designed by Ralph Adams Cram. Andrew Mellon, owner of Gulf Oil and ALCOA, donated funds to build a library and later his son Paul Mellon, Choate class of 1925, contributed a science laboratory. A gymnasium, athletic fields, and landscaping—designed by a Choate science

Choate Rosemary Hall
Hill House

Choate Rosemary Hall
Paul Mellon Arts Center

teacher and plantsman—completed St. John's vision for the campus. Several of the buildings were built by the school's own workforce and students helped plant the trees. By 1931, enrollment reached 510 boys, many of whom went on to attend prestigious eastern universities, particularly Yale University. Choate's athletic teams excelled in baseball, crew, and football, where a lasting rivalry with Deerfield Academy was born.

Back in Greenwich, although Rosemary Hall had rebounded to some extent from the crisis of 1948, the school entered the turbulent 1960s with shaky finances and dissension between the faculty and headmistress over racial integration. The growing trend toward coeducation in colleges motivated Rosemary Hall and Choate to explore a merger.[22] In 1968, the two schools agreed to move Rosemary Hall from Greenwich

Northfield Mount
Hermon School
Crossley Hall

back to Wallingford where a separate "upper campus" was built for the incoming girls. The upper campus, designed by James S. Polshek,[23] included dormitories, classrooms, a dining hall, gymnasium, and library. Most academic courses and extracurricular activities were shared with Choate. This arrangement—one version of coordinate education—lasted until 1978, when the two schools merged as Choate Rosemary Hall. The Paul Mellon Arts Center, sited and designed by the architect I. M. Pei, served as the "hub of the dual campus." It contains a large auditorium/theater with seating for the combined student population which numbered 800 students at the time. Of those students, approximately seventy-percent were boys. Twenty-five years later, enrollment had grown to over 1,000 students with approximately an equal number of boys and girls. Citing the objective of "preserving and extending Choate Rosemary Hall's historic commitment to excellence," the trustees voted to reduce the number of students to 825 while maintaining gender parity.[24] The downsizing allowed the former Rosemary Hall residential and student life facilities on the upper campus to be repurposed for administrative uses.

The trustees of Northfield and Mount Hermon, Abbot Academy and Andover, and other schools considering coeducation studied the Choate Rosemary Hall merger, both in the decision making process and the transition period.

NORTHFIELD AND MOUNT HERMON MERGER

The Reverend Dwight L. Moody, a Christian evangelist preacher, founded the Northfield Seminary for Young Ladies near his ancestral home in 1879. Northfield is located in the west highlands of the Connecticut River, a region of Massachusetts that is also home to Deerfield Academy and Smith, Mount Holyoke, and Amherst colleges. In 1881, Moody founded Mount Hermon School for Boys, about six miles south of Northfield in the east highlands of the river. At the time, Moody was in his forties. Twenty years prior, he had become a successful Chicago businessman and participated in evangelical revivals and missionary work. He established the Moody Bible Institute and the Illinois Street Church and preached the gospel around the country. Guided by his music director Ira Sanky, "the evangelist of song," he published hymnals and later used the royalties to help fund buildings on both campuses. They referred to the buildings as "sung-up."[25]

By the 1910s, both the Northfield and Mount Hermon campuses were fully developed. With gifts from gilded age benefactors—Mrs. Russell Sage, Cornelius Vanderbilt, Jay Gould's daughter Helen, and DeWitt Wallace—Moody was able to hire notable architectural firms that suited his eclectic stylistic preferences. Shepley, Rutan and Coolidge, Rand and Taylor, and Delano and Aldrich[26] designed buildings in styles ranging from delicate Queen Anne to massive Romanesque Revival. In 1894, the Auditorium building on the Northfield campus—designed by Fuller and Wheeler in an Italian Renaissance influenced style—opened to serve school assemblies but equally importantly, summer revival meetings. In the 1900s, Parish and Schroeder[27] designed five buildings on the Mount Hermon campus in a consistent and restrained Beaux-Arts style.

The first step toward unification was the 1912 creation of a single board of trustees formed to oversee both schools. Each school was run by its own principal, with a separate campus, faculty, and traditions. This form of governance prevailed until 1971, when Northfield and Mount Hermon merged under a single head of school. To accommodate an enrollment of about 1,100 students, the school maintained both campuses and shuttled faculty and students to classes and events.[28]

By the turn of the twentieth century, co-ordinate education was an anachronism and dual campuses had become prohibitively expensive to operate. A difficult emotional debate over which campus would be more suitable for consolidation continued for several years within the Northfield Mount Hermon community. The comparative cost of renovating existing and constructing new buildings—which favored Mount Hermon—was offset by the symbolic value of the Northfield campus, the Moody homestead and burial ground. In 2003, the trustees decided to sell the Northfield campus—retaining ownership of the Moody family properties and use of the Auditorium and other more public buildings—and consolidate on the Mount Hermon campus.[29] The decisive factor was that the Mount Hermon campus had the infrastructure: bedrock instead of sand, a central green instead of buildings that owed their siting to natural features, the Parish and Schroeder classical aesthetic, and room for expansion without compromising the whole.[30]

Downsizing accompanied consolidation. Today there are approximately 650 students on the Northfield Mount Hermon campus. To achieve consolidation, the school built two new cottage type dormitories, an arts center, and an admission office. In 2012, the Northfield campus was donated by the initial buyer to the National Christian Foundation (NCF) that sought a "long-term owner and occupant for the property that will honor the legacy of D. L. Moody."[31] In 2017, the foundation donated a portion of the campus lands and forty buildings to Thomas Aquinas College. The college, founded by the Roman Catholic Church in 1971, is located in Santa Paula, California. It plans to open the New England Campus in 2018.[32] The remaining acreage and 10 buildings were donated to the non-profit Moody Center, fulfilling the NCF's commitment to Moody's legacy.

The Hotchkiss School
Watson Hall

THE HOTCHKISS SCHOOL: ADMISSION OF GIRLS TO AN ALL-BOYS SCHOOL

Hotchkiss, founded in 1891 in the northwest corner of Connecticut, was in no position to merge with a nearby girls' school; there were none. Its neighbor, Kent School, had embarked on coordinate education in 1962. Kent built a separate campus for girls on Skiff Mountain and thirty years later consolidated the schools on the boys' Housatonic Valley campus. Hotchkiss, however, chose to achieve coeducation by admitting girls directly.[33]

The trustees appointed A. William "Bill" Olsen Jr. as headmaster in 1960 to succeed earlier twentieth-century legends known as "the King" and "the Duke." In the spring of 1970, the Hotchkiss trustees started considering options for achieving coeducation. Olsen's wife Jean, a Smith College graduate, was a champion of women's education. She surveyed the coeducation efforts at of other schools, including Exeter, Andover, St. Paul's, Choate, Kent, and Taft, and in the process gained admirers and detractors. One such detractor was Richard Gurney, a Hotchkiss English teacher and football coach from 1935 to 1971. Gurney, a holdover from the reign of the Duke, George van Santvoord, declared "if Hotchkiss ever became a coeducational school, Hotchkiss would be dead." In late 1972, however, the trustees voted to "take in girls."[34]

Olsen's job then became to implement the trustee's mandate. His "timetables and targets for coeducation" guided the process of transforming an all-male bastion into a more diverse environment.[35] The enrollment target was 500 students, phased in over three years. In 1974, the school would enroll 350 boys and 65 girls and over next three years, the number of boys would remain steady while the number of girls would increase to 150. Over time, the numbers of girls and boys would "seek their own level" which today is approximately 600 students, equally divided between the sexes. The expanded enrollment and admission of girls required more faculty, particularly women, and new and renovated buildings.

Mr. Olsen, with the Long-Range Planning Committee, hired architect Evans Woollen, class of 1945, to develop a master plan. The committee's academic priorities were an expanded library and new art facilities. Existing large dormitories would be renovated, and new ones designed, to produce "a more intimate familial life on a smaller scale." In converted bathrooms, for example, bathtubs would be added and urinals removed. The school built Watson Hall, the first dormitory specifically designed for girls, in 1979. The building is domestically scaled, and the rooms are single occupancy. A later girls' dormitory, Garland Hall, also contains all single rooms, but the massing and exterior elevations are updated Hotchkiss Georgian. In retrospect, the assumption that girls would prefer a more domestic environment than boys seems patronizing. The existing infirmary would be converted to a dormitory and an existing house renovated to serve health care needs. Woolen argued unsuccessfully for a "first-class" renovation of Bissell Hall, the original dormitory. Thirty years later, however, the building was demolished to create a site for a new dormitory quadrangle. Housing units for the expanded faculty would be carved out of existing dormitories and in newly-built single family houses. Lockers and showers for girls and an exercise area would be added to the existing gymnasium. As their twenty-fifth anniversary gift, the class of 1949 donated funds for additional athletic fields. Woolen proposed a new, larger library and to "backfill" the vacated space with art studios. Instead, the school expanded the library—by "interflooring" and an addition—and built a new wing for art studios.[36] To achieve these objectives, the trustees launched a $7.5 million, three-year, capital campaign.

SUMMARY

The whole student, once constrained by WASP mores, now embodies economic, racial, religious, and gender diversity. The next chapter continues this evolution by examining the body (athletics and health and wellness) and soul (religion, memorials) of the whole student.

Notes

1 - *Princeton Alumni Weekly* March 22, 2017 Volume 117, Number 9.

2 - *Choate Rosemary Hall: a history of the school*, page 175.

3 - *Lift Thine Eyes: the landscape, the buildings, the heritage of Northfield Mount Hermon School*, page 172.

4 - *After the Harkness Gift: a history of Phillips Exeter Academy since 1930* pages 153–5.

5 - http://privateschool/about.com/od/scholarships/a/A-Better-Chance.htm; accessed January 6, 2017.

6 - *After the Harkness Gift*, page 160.

7 - *Choate Rosemary Hall*, page 197.

8 - Exeter, for example, ended mandatory chapel in 1968 as did Deerfield in 1971. Choate Rosemary Hall removed the cross from its chapel in 1980.

9 - Deerfield had schooled boys and girls from its inception, but in 1948 it became an all-male school. It resumed admitting females in 1989.

10 - Other women's colleges included: Radcliffe, Smith, Wellesley, Bryn Mawr, Barnard, and Mount Holyoke. Other all-girls prep schools in New England included: Miss Porters (1843), The Masters School (1877), Dana Hall (1881), Miss Halls (1898), Westover (1909), and Ethel Walker (1911).

11 - *Wrought with steadfast will: a history of the Emma Willard School*, page 40.

12 - *Lift Thine Eyes*, pages 180–83.

13 - The statutory age of consent to sexual relations in New York State was reduced from eighteen to seventeen years in 1965. Mandatory reporting by school officials of child sexual abuse was enacted in 1969 and subsequently strengthened over the next thirty years.

14 - *Hotchkiss: a chronicle of an American School*, page 80.

15 - In response to litigation and publicity concerning sexual abuse and misconduct at some boarding schools, administrators commissioned third-party investigations and published their findings. Their reports, while distressing to read, placed the behavior in context with societal changes during this period. Compared with media coverage, the reports are non-sensational and oriented toward reform.

16 - *After the Harkness Gift*, pages 172–174.

17 - For criteria visit niche.com; the source of 70% of the data is the U.S. Department of Education, the rest by parent and student surveys.

18 - *Choate Rosemary Hall*, page 6. Caroline Ruutz-Rees was headmistress of Rosemary Hall from 1890 to 1938, and continued teaching there into the 1950s. She earned the Lady Literate Arts degree from University of St Andrews in Scotland, and a Ph.D. from Columbia University while headmistress. Her credo: "Tell the truth, shoot straight and respect the intellectual life."

19 - ibid., page 39.

20 - ibid., pages 115–20.

21 - ibid., page 71.

22 - ibid., pages 176–7.

23 - James Stewart Polshek (active 1950s–2010s) led the eponymous firm he founded in New York City for over 50 years. The firm designed buildings for institutional, cultural, and academic clients nationwide. He was the Dean of the Columbia University Graduate School of Architecture, Planning, and Preservation from 1972 to 1987.

24 - *Choate Rosemary Hall*, page 220; compared with enrollment figures from 1978, the year of the merger, today there are about 70 percent more girls and twenty-five percent fewer boys.

25 - *Lift Thine Eyes*, pages 38–40.

26 - Shepley Rutan Coolidge (active 1870s–present) is the successor firm to H. H. Richardson and is currently known as Shepley Bulfinch. During the firm's incarnation as Shepley Rutan Coolidge (1886–1915) they planned the new campus of Stanford University and designed the first of the River Houses at Harvard.

27 - Parish and Schroeder (active 1890s–1910s) designed buildings for academic clients including Teacher's College of Columbia University and Princeton University. It is likely they came to the attention of Dwight Moody through their mutual contacts at the YMCA.

28 - *Lift Thine Eyes*, page 219.

29 - ibid. page 186.

30 - Northfield advocates believe that the Northfield campus' buildings, although eclectic, are evocative of the late Victorian era. See Chapter Six for illustrations.

31 - nmhschool.org/about/history/thenorthfieldcampus, accessed 1/17/2018

32 - https://thomasaquinas.edu/newengland, accessed 1/17/2018.

33 - St. Paul's and Exeter, and later Lawrenceville and Deerfield also chose the direct, but gradual, admission of girls. Ironically, Deerfield had educated girls for almost one-hundred-fifty-years before it started admitting boys only in the late 1940s. Less than forty years later, Deerfield restored coeducation.

34 - *Hotchkiss: a chronicle of an American School*, pages 380–81.

35 - Revised summary of timetables and targets for coeducation. Hotchkiss archives, December 1, 1972.

36 - "Backfill" in campus planning terminology means to move a new use into a vacated space after the previous use is relocated. "Interfloor" means to insert an intermediate level, or mezzanine, between two floors where floor-to-floor height permits.

Phillips Academy Andover
Cochran Chapel

5: THE WHOLE STUDENT: BODY AND SOUL

The headmaster and the boy kept throwing the baseball at each other with everything they had. Finally, the boy quit. "Of course, I was wearing a glove and he wasn't," says the headmaster.
    John McPhee, *The Headmaster*

Therefore, every religious education must try to find the existentially important questions which are alive in the minds and hearts of the students
    Paul Tillich, Theology of Education St. Paul's School,
    1956 Academic Symposium The Church School in our Time

First, the body. Interscholastic sports among the Eight Schools were not organized until the 1880s. Before then, students played informal games on nearby fields and bodies of water. The College of New Jersey (now Princeton University) and Rutgers College (now Rutgers University) played the first intercollegiate football game in 1869.[1] Following their lead, Exeter and Andover played the first interscholastic football game in 1878.[2] Today, the Eight Schools on average deploy about thirty teams—boys and girls, varsity and junior varsity—over three seasons. And, of course, they compete with one another, giving rise to rivalries such as Deerfield versus Choate, and Exeter versus Andover. The schools built their first indoor gymnasiums in the 1880s, mainly for winter exercise. Frank Boyden's "athletics for all" echoes the progressive principle of educating the whole student.[3] Participation in sports channels teenage energy into healthy competition, teaches teamwork, and builds friendships. The advent of female athletes in the 1970s required schools to enlarge their coaching staffs, locker rooms, playing fields, and gyms.

While athletics enable healthier lifestyles, injuries put the burden on schools to care for injured athletes. Infirmaries had first appeared on campuses in the mid-1800s in response to the threat of contagious diseases.[4] Yellow fever, cholera, and scarlet fever, among others, disrupted daily activities and claimed lives in nineteenth-century America. Epidemics continue to threaten society, but twentieth-century advances in epidemiology and public health initiatives have reduced the need for in-patient care. Boarding schools used this opportunity to convert infirmaries to dormitories and to develop an alternative building type, the health and wellness center. In addition to treating routine medical needs, these centers provide education in life-style issues such

Choate Rosemary Hall
The Big Gym

Phillips Exeter Academy
The Old Gym

as sexually transmitted diseases, drug and alcohol abuse, smoking, and bullying.

Care of the soul, or spirituality, is another aspect of the whole student. Each of the Eight Schools was founded and led, until recently, by a Protestant clergyman. Exeter, Andover, Deerfield, and Hotchkiss adhered to the Congregational faith. Choate, Rosemary Hall, and St. Paul's followed the Episcopalian tradition.[5] Lawrenceville was Presbyterian and Northfield and Mount Hermon were Evangelical. The Northfield campus was home to spiritual summer conferences in the late nineteenth century.[6] As Jewish, Roman Catholic, and students from other religious traditions enrolled, the Protestant Christian ethic no longer represented the entire community. In the 1970s, students of many faith backgrounds rebelled against compulsory chapel attendance and argued for an ecumenical approach to theology. They posted articles in student newspapers and petitioned the administration and Trustees to address their concerns.[7] Each school responded in its own way, but by the end of the 1970s, most had moved to voluntary attendance at daily services and some even at Sunday services. Schools initiated multi-cultural and artistic programs to fill the void. Some longstanding traditions, such as Deerfield's Sunday evening sing, have been maintained.

Spirituality becomes tangible when students, alumni, or faculty are killed serving their country in the military. Following the Civil War, World War I, World War II, the war in southeast Asia, and more recent conflicts, the school community—often led by alumni—came together to establish memorials. These took the form of named buildings, towers, monuments, and landscapes. Most alumni societies were formed for this purpose and have grown to provide additional support to their alma mater, particularly in fund raising.

The following sections illustrate how the body and soul aspects of the whole student are revealed in the campus buildings and grounds.

Phillips Exeter Academy
Love Gymnasium

ATHLETIC FACILITIES

Phillips Exeter Academy, founded in 1781, did not build its first proper gymnasium until 1885. In prior years, gymnastic equipment was occasionally set up outdoors and later in space rented in a storefront across the street from campus. The Old Gym was located near the main Academy Building and contained a baseball practice room (or cage), an elevated running track, locker room, and several bowling alleys. It was a handsome two-story brick building, with a turret, arched openings, and articulated chimney.[8]

In the early twentieth century, the campus expanded across Front Street to the south with construction of two dormitories and a library. Further south, Thompson Gym—the first building on today's athletic campus—was built in 1918. Designed by Cram and Ferguson in the fashionable Beaux-Arts style, the gym contained a swimming pool and a large open space with high ceilings for track and baseball practice. The gym also served as a venue for film screenings, a rarity at the time. The gym was set among undeveloped fields, known at the time as the Sunday Campus. Students snuck off there on Sunday afternoons to escape a prohibition against sporting activities on the Christian sabbath. Some speculate the Sunday Campus served as inspiration for scenes in the book *A Separate Peace* by John Knowles, Exeter class of 1945.[9]

In 1969, adjacent to Thompson Gym, the school built a much larger gym containing a competition pool, two hockey rinks, three basketball courts, twelve squash courts, and support facilities. The first unabashedly modern building on campus, the roof is supported by long span exterior steel trusses. The current South Campus master plan indicates an expansion of the Love Gymnasium with a new field house that provides more all-weather spaces for recreation and fitness, as well as varsity and JV teams. The master plan also includes a new building for the Department of Theater and Dance, including classrooms, rehearsal rooms, and two performance stages.[10] Both buildings, the field house—designed by

THE WHOLE STUDENT: BODY AND SOUL

St. Paul's School
Lower School Pond
c. 1890

ARC/Architectural Resources Cambridge—and the performing arts building—designed by Williams and Tsien—are exemplars of contemporary architectural design.

Before gymnasiums, students played informal games and competitive sports outdoors. Land was plentiful and no school is far from a lake or river. Today, dedicated playing fields and, in some cases, golf courses provide ample opportunity for students to engage in intramural and interscholastic sports. Entering students are assigned to athletic clubs—such as Delphians, Isthmians, and Old Hundreds at St. Paul's—and every student engages daily in some team activity. Through training and talent, the better student-athletes play interscholastic sports, a credential that enhances their college applications.

Students at St. Paul's School, with easy access to several ponds, started playing hockey on the ice and rowing on the water in the early years of the school. St. Paul's reputation as "the cradle of American hockey" is well-deserved, since the first ice hockey game in the United States was played there in 1884.[11] The sport was so popular that at one time there were nine rinks in use on the Lower School pond. Hobey Baker, form of 1908, excelled in hockey both at St. Paul's and later Princeton University. His skates were fitted with silver blades. The availability of "artificial ice"—produced by circulating refrigerant in pipes below the surface—extended the season. In 1952, a permanent rink was built using this technology and in 1966 it was roofed over. In 1999, David Ingalls Jr.—St. Paul's class of 1952—donated funds for construction of an additional rink, named after his father, who previously had donated funds for Ingalls Rink at Yale. The two combined rinks, with team and spectator amenities, are located on the shore of the Lower School pond.

Rowing, or crew, is another popular outdoor sport at St. Paul's. The rowing teams—

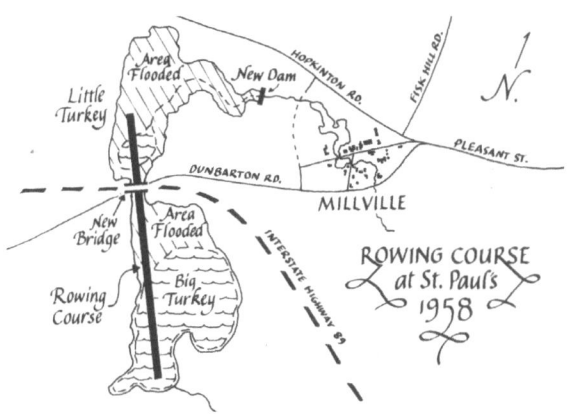

St Paul's School
Rowing Course 1958

St. Paul's School
Rowing Course 1958

interscholastic and club—practice and race on the Turkey ponds just southwest of campus. The earliest, informal races were held on the Lower School pond, but in 1871, they moved to Long Pond, the town reservoir.[12] As the sport and Concord (the town) grew, the school was forced to look for another venue. The next closest body of water on school property is Little Turkey pond, but it was not large or deep enough for regattas. Coincidentally, in the 1950s, the federal government was planning the right-of-way for a new interstate highway, I-89. The school traded sixty acres of land to the government in return for a channel joining Little Turkey with Great Turkey ponds, and a bridge to span the channel. By damming the Turkey River downstream of Little Turkey pond, St. Paul's was able to create a 2,000-meter course. The first regatta on the new course was held in 1958.

In addition to ice hockey and crew, the Eight Schools provide playing fields for football, track, soccer, lacrosse, field hockey, baseball and softball, and tennis courts. Some of Deerfield's ninety acres of playing fields are located in the flood plain of the Deerfield River. Some years, in the spring, the river inundates the fields and students take advantage of the opportunity to play unconventional water sports. The school's baseball diamond, however, is located on the plateau above the flood plain, amid academic and student life buildings. It is named Headmaster's Field in honor of Frank Boyden.

INFIRMARIES

In March through November 1918, a nationwide influenza epidemic killed over 500,000 people, including several at The Lawrenceville School. One was the head of school, Simon John McPherson, a medical doctor. He contracted the deadly disease while treating afflicted students.[13] The trustees and parents responded to this tragedy by

The Lawrenceville
School
McPhearson Hall

The Lawrenceville
School
Rashid Health and
Wellness Center

building an infirmary in his honor. Infirmaries of this vintage provided convalescence for sick students and quarantine from the rest of the school community. Lawrenceville's two-story, Colonial Revival building, designed by Delano and Aldrich, opened in 1929 during the polio epidemic. The two large faceted bays on the eastern end of the building, called solariums, allowed patients to benefit from outdoor air and sunlight. Like other Eight Schools in the 1970s, Lawrenceville built a new health and wellness center and converted the infirmary into a dormitory. Patient rooms became dorm rooms and the solariums became social spaces. The Al Rashid Health and Wellness Center provides health education, sports medicine, and psychological counseling, as well as traditional out-patient and limited in-patient services. The building is on a site and designed in a style that creates an aesthetic bridge between the late nineteenth-century Circle houses and the late twentieth-century Crescent houses.

St Paul's School
Chapel of
St. Peter and St. Paul

CHAPELS

The Eight Schools gave prominence to their chapels, both in siting and design. Many of the late nineteenth-and-early twentieth-century's best architects were awarded these prestigious commissions.[14] The Chapel of St. Peter and St. Paul at St. Paul's School, designed by Henry Vaughn[15] and built in 1888, was anointed "for American prep schools, the mother of all chapels" by the architectural critic Robert Campbell.[16] In fact, the mother of that chapel is the original Chapel of St. Paul designed by George Snell in 1858. Both buildings are first rank examples of Gothic Revival architecture. Upon receipt of a new organ in 1929 and an enrollment increase, the larger chapel was expanded in a most unusual way. The sanctuary—housing the altar at the far eastern end of the building—was moved forward far enough to insert two new bays.[17] Deftly designed by Cram and Ferguson and their structural engineers, the resulting building appears seamless, one of the seams being concealed in the wall of a new choir room.

The interior of the chapel is richly ornamented, including a sculpture by Daniel Chester French memorializing members of the St. Paul's community who died in World War One. The reredos, an elaborately carved wooden screen placed behind the altar, was given by Mr. and Mrs. Cornelius Vanderbilt in memory of their son, William, class of 1899. The stained glass windows were given in memory of various figures, including a rector (head of school) and a faculty member. A twenty-three bell carillon was installed in 1933 in the tower—part of Vaughn's original design—that had been added to the building in 1894.[18]

Just as chapel buildings were adapted to accommodate changing needs, after World War Two the place of organized religion—particularly in a church school such as St. Paul's—was

St. Paul's School
Chapel enlargement 1928

changing. An Academic Symposium, on the subject "The Church School in Our Time," was convened during St. Paul's centennial in 1956. At the symposium, the Reverend Paul Tillich, a theologian, philosopher, and author, gave the keynote address titled "The Theology of Education." Going back to the Middle Ages, Tillich identified three types of education: technical, humanistic, and inducting. These types are analogous to Aristotle's three philosophies: natural, mental, and moral. To paraphrase Tillich, with apologies to Aristotle, the technical/natural aims to provide "training in basic and specialist skills," the humanistic/mental aims to enable a student to actualize his or her own potential, and the inducting/moral aims to impart values, customs, practices, and faith, and to provide an "initiation into the mystery of human existence." Tillich believed the problem, in his time, lay in "the conflict between inducting and humanistic education" and concluded that "the problem is infinite and must be solved in every generation again."[19] Tillich's generation, however, was on the cusp of a secular revolution, where the problem he identified became an anachronism.

What did this revolution mean for campus churches and church schools? Today, St. Paul's conducts all-school gatherings in the chapel four mornings a week. With input from students, programs of music, talks, and spiritual reflections are offered. Traditional Episcopal services are held three times a week and are open to the public as well as to students on a voluntary basis. There are student-led faith groups organized around particular interests and practices including: charismatic Christian, interfaith, Jewish Hillel, an Indian Society (Buddhist, Hindu and Muslim faiths), a Middle Eastern Society, Roman Catholic, and the longstanding Missionary Society. Matthew Warren, the seventh rector of the school, believed that "it was in chapel that the polarities of old and new, of tradition and change, could be reconciled."[20] His belief, stated in the 1970s, holds true today—at least at St. Paul's.

While some other schools no longer offer traditional services in their chapels, they have re-purposed their buildings for more broadly spiritual, secular, and multi-cultural activities.

WAR MEMORIALS

Beginning with the Civil War, alumni, faculty, and some students served in the military. To memorialize those who died in wartime, schools—often led by alumni—raised funds to erect towers, name buildings, and plant landscapes. The Memorial Bell Tower at Andover, for example, designed by Guy Lowell,[21] was built in 1923 in memory of those Andover men who died in World War One. The selected site, on the southeast corner of the intersection of Main and Salem Streets, is signif-icant for several reasons. First, it is the highest point on Academy Hill. Second,

Phillips Academy Andover
Memorial Bell Tower

Deerfield Civil War Monument (left)
Brick Church (right)

the site is across Salem Street from the original Academy building of 1786. Third, the ground was used for militia training during the Revolutionary War and reportedly visited by George Washington after the war.[22] Lastly, the site served as a foothold in the tug-of-war to determine which side of Main Street would be developed for campus growth. Lowell placed the tower in the middle of the site and surrounded it with a plaza. The 160-foot high tower is twenty-feet square in plan and features a limestone base, a brick shaft divided in three sections by belt courses, and an elaborate wooden tiered spire containing a thirty-seven bell carillon.

At Mount Hermon, the school planted two closely-spaced, semi-circular rows of American white pine trees in honor of the sixty-nine alumni who died in World War I. On Round Top, "the most sacred spot" on the Northfield campus, twenty-six spruce trees were planted in 1920 to honor missionaries who died in foreign countries. These landscape memorials are characteristic of a school that celebrates its natural setting in many ways. The Civil War monument on Deerfield's town common—the site of the stockade erected for protection by the original settlers—is characteristic of the close historic relationship between the town and the academy.

On the campuses of Deerfield and Hotchkiss, town cemeteries preceded the founding of the schools. Today, as a result, the cemeteries—like Grove Street Cemetery at Yale University—are embedded in their campuses. While cemeteries are historically significant, they present impediments to campus growth. At Deerfield, the cemetery borders several dormitories and the western wing of the athletic complex. At Hotchkiss, several dormitories surround the cemetery. In 1810, Andover built the chapel cemetery in a wooded area with grave sites reserved for deceased members of the seminary and academy community. Today it is surrounded with dormitory and academic buildings.

SUMMARY

From playing catch with the headmaster to discovering the "existentially important questions," a student must navigate an array of challenges and possibilities presented to him/her during the four—more or less—years of a prep school education. Having probed the four aspects of the whole student in this and the previous three chapters, the next three chapters explore the whole campus: place, planning, and architecture.

Notes

1 - *Princeton and Rutgers: the two colonial colleges in New Jersey,* page 53.

2 - *The Phillips Exeter Academy: a pictorial history,* page 47.

3 - *The Headmaster: Frank L. Boyden of Deerfield,* page 15.

4 - *A Brief History of St. Paul's School,* page 25.

5 - Other Episcopal church schools in New England include: St. Mark's, founded in 1868, Groton in 1884, St. George's in 1896, and Kent in 1906.

6 - Summer conferences, part of the widespread popularity of camp meetings and revivals, required large dormitories and meeting halls, precipitating a building boom at Northfield.

7 - *Deerfield 1797–2007: a pictorial history of the academy,* page 162.

8 - *The Phillips Exeter Academy: a pictorial history,* page 54.

9 - Exeter Bulletin 2011

10 - Exeter Bulletin 2015

11 - Saint Paul's School Sesquicentennial Exhibition, sps.edu, Ohrstrom Library.

12 - *A Brief History of St. Paul's School,* pages 17–19.

13 - *The Lawrenceville School: a bicentennial portrait,* page 20.

14 - Chapel commissions were awarded to: Peabody & Stearns at Lawrenceville; Shepley, Rutan and Coolidge at Northfield; Ralph Adams Cram at Choate and Exeter; Charles Platt at Andover; and Delano and Aldrich at Hotchkiss.

15 - Henry Vaughn (active 1880s–1910s) specialized in designing Gothic Revival Episcopal churches, including The Washington National Cathedral, St. John the Divine in New York City, Trinity Church on the Green in New Haven, and parish churches across the northeast.

16 - *Architectural Record*, 1999.

17 - The original chapel was also enlarged using a similar method, although at a much smaller scale.

18 - *St. Paul's: the life of a New England school*, pages 217–221.

19 - The full text of Tillich's address is archived in the Ohrstrom Library at St. Paul's School.

20 - *St. Paul's: the life of a New England school*, pages 306–7.

21 - Guy Lowell (active 1900s–1920s) was trained at the École des Beaux-Arts. Upon starting his practice in Boston, he blended elements of Academic Classicism and Georgian Revival for buildings at Harvard and Brown Universities. He was the campus architect for Andover before yielding to Charles Platt.

22 - *Academy Hill: the Andover campus, 1778 to the present*, page 117.

View from Mount Holyoke, Northampton, Massachusetts, after a Thunderstorm—The Oxbow, 1836
Thomas Cole

6: THE WHOLE CAMPUS: NATURAL SETTING AND TOWN

Green fields and trees, streams and ponds, beautiful scenery, flowers and minerals, are educators.

George Shattuck founder of St Paul's [1]

Moody possessed an orthodox Christian understanding of nature. For him, God's creation testified to the Creator. [2]

These beliefs—professed by the founders of St. Paul's School, Northfield Seminary, and Mount Hermon School in the mid-1800s—reflected the Transcendentalist principle that direct observation of nature was the key to learning and godliness.[3] This principle had been articulated in the early 1800s by authors such as Henry David Thoreau in his book *Walden*, and painters of the Hudson River School such as Thomas Cole. Andrew Jackson Downing's[4] book *Treatise on the Theory and Practice of Landscape Gardening*, published in 1841, applied this principle to architectural and landscape design. Downing, who designed country houses and their grounds in a picturesque style, influenced a generation of designers including Frederick Law Olmsted.

The Transcendentalist attitude, nurtured in more arcadian times, came into conflict with the realities of nineteenth-century urban life. In the early 1800s, wealthy urban New England families, seeking to escape increasing congestion, pollution, and crime, built country estates for leisure and kept townhouses in the city for business and socializing. Later in the century, facilitated by advances in commuter transportation, garden suburbs—again populated by prosperous families—arose adjacent to large cities. Brookline, for example, a suburb of Boston, came under pressure for development in the late nineteenth century. Streets and streetcars emanating from the city center extended into Brookline and beyond.[5] Rising land values made subdividing large estates attractive to property owners and developers. What distinguished Brookline from neighboring areas was the presence of landscape architects such as Frederick Law Olmsted and his sons, who established permanent residence there in 1895. They designed Brookline's infrastructure, plotted subdivisions, and served on the planning board.

Impressive single-family homes were built in the choicest locations, primarily on the several hills that graced the town. From the 1880s to the 1930s, Brookline was home of many of the architects and planners who designed buildings on campuses of the Eight Schools. In addition to the Olmsteds, who had commissions for projects at Lawrenceville, St. Paul's, Deerfield, and Andover, these included: Robert Peabody and John Stearns, who designed projects at Lawrenceville and Deerfield; Ernest Bowditch, campus planner at Hotchkiss; George Shepley, and George Rutan, projects at Northfield Seminary; Guy Lowell, at Andover; and Robert Andrews and Herbert Jacques at Abbott Academy.[6] They transposed the land planning strategies and aesthetic of Brookline to the campuses of their clients.

Scholarly and professional interest in the natural environment blossomed in late nineteenth century in the United States, partly as an antidote to the increasing disregard for—and destruction of—that environment. Natural history museums, such as the University Museum at Harvard, and arboretums, such as the Arnold Arboretum in Boston, inspired collaboration among architects, landscape designers, and their clients. Charles Sprague Sargent, the first director of the Arnold Arboretum, advanced "the free-flowing, naturalistic planting and design approach that came down to him through the writings of Andrew Jackson Downing."[7] The arboretum, designed by Sargent in collaboration with Frederick Law Olmsted beginning in 1872, became a resource for Harvard's School of Landscape Architecture, founded in 1900.[8] Another indication of the profession's growing importance was the founding of the American Society of Landscape Architects in 1899.

The twentieth-century's relentless drive toward industrialization and urbanism—and modern architecture's ahistorical polemics and preference for abstract composition—relegated nature and landscape planning to the background. Farms were turned into housing developments; scenic areas and historic sites were disrupted by interstate highways; rivers were diverted and dammed; and air, water, and soil were polluted. The first Earth Day in 1970, however, marked a resurgence of awareness of the natural environment and its interaction with humankind. Ian McHarg's[9] book *Design With Nature* was a wake-up call for the design professions. Sustainability became a key objective of building and site design and was codified in 2000 by the Leadership in Energy and Environmental Design (LEED) certification system.[10] This chapter explores the interaction of the natural and built environments on several Eight Schools campuses.

NATURAL LANDSCAPE

Dr. George Shattuck, Jr., a Boston physician and the founder of St. Paul's School, purchased a country home and farm in Millville west of Concord, New Hampshire, in 1855. A mill had been established in the late eighteenth century at a falls of the Turkey River, where a dam was built to power the mill and create mill ponds upstream. Now part of the school, the ponds are named after adjacent buildings: the Lower School, since demolished, and the Library, since relocated. The property, although only three miles from Concord, seems rustic now as it did then. The topography is rugged, dotted with abandoned stone quarries in the vicinity, and views in the distance of the Franconia Mountains to the north and Mount Monadnock to the southwest.[11] The St. Paul's School campus, surrounded by more than 2,000 wooded acres, is one of the most naturally beautiful.

After the initial forty years of unplanned growth, an alumni group commissioned Olmsted

St. Paul's School
Stream Valley Below
Dam

St. Paul's School
Aeriel View of Campus
Looking Northwest

Brothers to report on possible ways to organize and expand the campus. Historically, main street is the dominant, or default, organizing element of New England towns. St. Paul's original buildings were sited along Dunbarton Road, a country thoroughfare that traversed the campus. Olmsted Brothers' report, however, concluded that since the land on the east side of the road fell away precipitously into the stream valley, a one-sided village street could not provide a cohesive structure. Next, they looked at the ponds, which, as Thoreau once observed of lakes, are "a landscape's

THE WHOLE CAMPUS: NATURAL SETTING AND TOWN

Northfield Mount Hermon School
Connecticut River Looking South

Northfield Mount Hermon School
Looking West

most beautiful and expressive feature." The Olmsteds rejected the ponds as an organizing element because their size and location would require unacceptable separation of one building from another. Instead they focused their attention on the stream valley. They recommended trimming trees to open up views, removing old wooden buildings, and restoring an overgrown meadow. There was one problem: the stream served as the school's sewer discharge.

In 1923, the trustees commissioned Olmsted Brothers, with the architect Grosvenor Atterbury, to conduct a more extensive study. By then, Dunbarton Road had been realigned by the county and the sewage treated differently. Their study recommended a concentration of teaching facilities and a distribution of housing, arranged both formally and informally. The consensus was that informally was better suited to the topography. Today, all three organizing strategies are evident: the old road, the ponds, and the stream valley. The impact of the natural setting remains the dominant theme of campus development.

Another campus developed in close relation with a natural landscape is that of Northfield Mount Hermon. Today, the school is consolidated on one campus—the former boys school campus, Mount Hermon—but when founded by Dwight L. Moody in 1879–81, the girls and boys schools were separate. Northfield—the former girls school campus—is located on the east bank of the Connecticut River and Mount Hermon on the west side, some six miles downriver. The Connecticut River forms the border between Vermont and New Hampshire, then traverses Massachusetts and Connecticut, and finally empties into Long Island Sound at Old Saybrook. The river valley in central Massachusetts where Moody selected sites for his schools—north of the vantage point of Thomas Cole's painting—is particularly scenic. There are wide flood plains on either bank, hills descending to the flood plains, and mountain ranges in the distance. Given the meandering course of the river and the prevailing winds, the Northfield campus is underlain with sand, while Mount Hermon's substrate is rock.

Northfield Mount Hermon School Aerial View of the Northfield Seminary campus looking East 1913

Northfield Mount Hermon School Aerial View of the Mount Hermon Campus Looking West 1913

By the 1910s—a span of thirty years since the founding—both campuses were fully developed. Moody had read Downing's treatise on cottage design and picturesque landscape. The architects he selected—including Rand and Taylor, Fuller and Wheeler, and Parish and Schroeder—were attuned to the natural setting and Downing's theory of the picturesque.[12] They sited buildings to fit within the rolling contours and to take advantage of the proximate and distant views. The original buildings at Northfield were oriented toward the sunset, and Mount Hermon's toward the sunrise.[13] They laid out curving roads and paths, planted specimen trees on sloping lawns, and placed memorials on promontories.

Today, the long vehicular approach to the combined Northfield Mount Hermon campus meanders through a forest, past a lake, and arrives at the original cottage row on Grass Hill. The cottages, dining hall, student center, and chapel sit on a north-south ridge facing the river valley. Academic buildings step downhill in an irregular east-west line. On the next tier, loosely arranged around athletic fields that

THE WHOLE CAMPUS: NATURAL SETTING AND TOWN

Northfield Mount
Hermon School
Consolidated
Campus Aerial View
Looking South

were once wetlands are a gymnasium and an arts center. The arts center replaced the original classroom and science buildings that were destroyed by fire. Still further down the hill, closer to the river, are the hockey rink and boathouse.

The Northfield campus is linked to the town's main street and the Moody birthplace. The earliest buildings (1880–95) gently flow down the hills and spread out over the landscape. Designed in late Victorian masonry style with towers, gables, and steep roofs, they appear even taller than their three-and-four-story massing would suggest. There were several attempts between 1907 and 1923 by Charles Lowrie[14] to impose axial symmetry, quadrangles, and other Beaux-Arts planning concepts on both campuses. Lowrie's plans were not implemented, in part due to the intervention of the Great Depression and both World Wars.[15]

CONSTRUCTED LANDSCAPE

Where a natural landscape offered few clues for siting buildings, land planners and architects creatively constructed landscapes. They designed open spaces framed by buildings, used various rectilinear and curvilinear geometric shapes to define precincts, laid out walkways to relate one building—or group of buildings—to another, enhanced streams to create ponds, drained or filled swamps—today's wetlands—to create usable land, regraded flat land to create landforms, extended existing patterns of buildings, and planted trees and gardens in various configurations.

Frederick Law Olmsted's plan for the Lawrenceville School in the late 1800s is an example of a constructed landscape. Olmsted and architect Robert Peabody used a circle as an organizing element. Olmsted envisioned the campus as parklike setting for Peabody's buildings and as

The Lawrenceville School
The Circle

The Lawrenceville School
1992 Master Plan
Prentice & Chan,
Ohlhausen

an outdoor classroom, a pedagogical landscape for students and teachers.[16] His planting plan specified and located over 370 species of deciduous, evergreen, and flowering trees. He specified labels for all the trees, much like an arboretum, but the labels gradually disappeared due to natural causes and vandalism. The trees themselves suffered from storms, disease, and inattention until 1954, when an endowment was funded to ensure that proper care would be provided for the grounds. New buildings and precincts—the Bowl in the 1920s, the Crescent in the 1980s, the Triangle in the 1990s, and Flagpole Green in the 2010s—were occasions to extend and adapt Olmsted's plan.

The dramatic reconfiguration of the

THE WHOLE CAMPUS: NATURAL SETTING AND TOWN

The Hotchkiss School
Lakeville Town Cemetery With Bissell
Family Gravestone

campus of Phillips Academy Andover in the 1920s is another example of a constructed landscape. Charles Platt, with assistance from Olmsted Brothers, superimposed a formal Beaux-Arts inspired plan over a landscape that had evolved incrementally over 125 years.

THE TOWN, THE LAND, AND THE CAMPUS

The founder of each of the Eight Schools wanted to locate their campus apart from the city but also within or near a small town. The late eighteenth-century schools—Andover, Exeter, and Deerfield—and Lawrenceville are embedded in and named after a town. As the towns and campuses grew, they strove, not always amicably, to achieve a balance between each other's needs. Other schools—Choate and Northfield—are located on the periphery of town. Still others—St. Paul's, Mount Hermon, and Hotchkiss—are more remote. Because the towns pre-dated the schools, the schools accommodated themselves to existing conditions, particularly roads and cemeteries. Roads can be realigned, as seen at St. Paul's and Hotchkiss, but cemeteries are sacred ground. As a result, Mary Bissell Hotchkiss' family plot in the Lakeville town cemetery is surrounded by dormitories. Expansion of Deerfield's and Andover's campuses is partially constrained by colonial-era town burying grounds.

For small towns and rural campuses in the eighteenth century, getting there from more populated areas was a challenge. Before train service, students arrived in horse and buggy. Roads were unpaved and bridges were few. The benefactors of Rosemary Hall—whose daughters attended the school when it was located in Wallingford—enticed Ms. Ruutz-Rees, the principal, to relocate the school to their home town of Greenwich for this very reason. In the mid-1800s, railroads extended to rural towns, making schools more accessible to a wider range of students. Students traveling to Mount Hermon rode a train to the local station and walked the remaining mile to campus.[17] The Connecticut River crossing was by ferry until a bridge was built in 1899. Eventually automobiles replaced the horse and buggy, although Frank Boyden, headmaster of Deerfield, preferred his buggy until he retired in 1968. With increasing traffic, schools had to provide parking as well as access for emergency and service vehicles. Interstate highways enabled long distance travel but, in some cases, threatened the rural character of campus. St. Paul's made a deal with transportation planners to provide a right-of-way through school land in exchange for dredging a channel and building a bridge that created an improved rowing course. Trans-Atlantic ships and, later, global airlines provided opportunity for local students to travel abroad and for international student to attend prep school in America in greater numbers.

School-owned property tends to be more extensive than the land on which the campus is built, known as the active campus. The need for land is driven by various factors, among them: a land bank for future expansion; development of athletic fields; a buffer zone from surrounding private development; and conservation purposes. Over time, contiguous land tends to become available in smaller parcels, at a higher price, and with more land use regulations. The original campuses of Choate, Rosemary Hall, and Hotchkiss were built on farmland owned for generations by the founders. Andover's trustees seized the opportunity to expand their campus when the adjacent seminary abruptly moved and put their buildings and grounds up for sale. Similarly, Lawrenceville purchased an adjacent farm when it came on the market in 1895 and built a golf course on the farmland the following year.[18]

Hotchkiss started with a relatively small campus but expanded as contiguous land became available. The original campus was built in the 1890s on sixty-five acres donated by the school's namesake. The site, located at the intersection of two country roads, has many amenities including a lake, rolling hills, and mountain views. A nine-hole golf course, originally built in 1911 but redesigned in 1925 with "roller coaster fairways and wildly contoured greens," encircles the core campus.[19] In the 1920s, the school purchased 200 acres of contiguous woodland that provided access to another lake, a parcel for a stadium and track, and an abundance of natural features for study and recreation. Then, in 2004, an alumnus donated 260 acres of farmland contiguous to both the woods and the main campus. The school uses the farm as a source of "real food"—local, ethical, and sustainable—for the dining hall, classes for environmental science, and opportunities for students to work in the fields and in the barn. Today, a seven-mile walking trail connects all three land holdings.

SCHOOL FARM

Agricultural production has also had an impact on school's land use and relationship to the land. In their early years, schools ran their own farms and patronized local farmers to supply food for their dining halls. In the second half of the nineteenth century, state land grant colleges—funded from the sale of federal lands—developed the science of farming. Through their research, food production was industrialized. Food distribution expanded nationwide by railroad and, later, by trucking and air freight. School farms became obsolete and their agricultural fields were converted to playing fields and other uses or left fallow. Then, in the 1960s, heightened awareness of the risks posed by some industrialized agriculture—particularly the use of chemical fertilizers and pesticides as documented in Rachael Carson's book *Silent Spring*—inspired a return to organic methods of farming. Beginning in the 1970s, the environmental movement created renewed academic interest in agriculture and fostered a hands-on opportunity for students.

The history of Northfield Mount Hermon's school farm illustrates this cycle of farm-to-fork and back again. When Dwight Moody purchased a 250-acre farm and started his school in one of the barns, he put boys to work cultivating fields and milking cows. By 1890, the school offered courses in agriculture, horticulture, animal husbandry, and dairying.[20] The farm produced an "internationally famous" Holstein herd, consisting of 375 cows and bulls. The bulls, used for breeding, and the cows, used for milk, generated revenue. A creamery supplied dairy products to the school and local families. In 1928, however, the school discontinued the agricultural courses to focus on liberal arts. In 1961, the school shut down the farm, but in 1975, it was revived by request of students. Today, they pro-

Choate Rosemary Hall
Kohler Environmental
Center

duce apple cider, maple syrup, honey, vegetables, milk, cheese, ice cream, and fruit jam for school use and for sale. In 2001, the "teaching farm" received an organic certification.

SUSTAINABLE DESIGN

The environmental movement also stimulated a holistic approach to the design and use of buildings and to site design and conservation. *Fast Company* characterized the Kohler Environmental Center at Choate Rosemary Hall as "SimCity meets Survivor: Wallingford." [21] The center, designed by Robert A. M. Stern Associates, opened in 2012. It is a unique blend of teaching, research, and residential spaces. About twenty fifth and sixth form students (juniors and seniors) and two faculty live at the center for one academic year. The complex features a dormitory with kitchen and common space; classrooms and laboratories; a greenhouse; and the surrounding natural environment for study and experimentation. While located in 266 acres of fields and forest, the center is close enough for residents to travel by bicycle or shuttle bus to the main campus for other school activities.

The complex was designed to operate at "net zero," meaning that it consumes no more energy than it produces. A one-acre solar panel array is designed to produce one-hundred-percent of the building's electrical needs. Rooftop solar tubes provide hot water. Waste water and kitchen waste are recycled. These features helped the project receive LEED Platinum status, the highest category achievable. Attaining the net zero goal, however, is determined as much by how residents use the building as by the efficacy of the various technical features. Residents monitor their energy usage and compete in teams to achieve the smallest environmental footprint. The author of the *Fast Company* article wonders "how far a group of motivated teenagers will go to win. Will they figure out a way to sell excess energy to rival Deerfield Academy?" [22]

SUMMARY

In the world-view of early nineteenth-century America, unspoiled nature embodied educational and spiritual values. As the century progressed, scholarly and scientific research expanded an understanding of natural phenomena but also accelerated a drive for development. The effort by campus planners and architects to maintain a balance between the natural environment as a preserve and as a resource continues to this day. The next chapter looks at land planning as a tool for responsible development.

Notes

1 - *A Brief History of St. Paul's School*, page 4.

2 - *Lift Thine Eyes*, page 62.

3 - *American Boarding Schools*, page 171.

4 - Andrew Jackson Downing (active 1840s–1852) lived in the Hudson Valley, home to the Hudson River School of painters and artisans. His interest in horticulture led to a career as a landscape gardener, author, and collaborator with architect Andrew Jackson Davis. With Davis, he authored *Cottage Residences*, a pattern book largely in the Gothic Revival style. He was editor of *The Horticulturist* magazine until his death.

5 - *Community By Design*, pages 137–167.

6 - ibid. page 237.

7 - ibid. page 134.

8 - The Yale University School of Forestry was also established in 1900. Environmental Studies was added to curriculum in 1971.

9 - Ian McHarg (active 1950s–1990s) was a professor of landscape architecture at the University of Pennsylvania and principal of an environmental planning and landscape architectural firm in Philadelphia. He championed a sustainable approach to development of land resources.

10 - Leadership in Energy and Environmental Design (LEED) is a certification program of the United States Green Building Council intended to encourage sustainable building design. Buildings are rated from Certified to Platinum based on the number of points achieved in various categories such as energy performance, indoor air quality, materials and resources, sustainable sites, and design innovation.

11 - *A Brief History of St. Paul's School*, page 7.

12 - *Lift Thine Eyes*, pages 62–65.

13 - ibid. page 26. Both campuses are oriented to the river.

14 - Charles Lowrie (active 1890s–1930s) was a charter member of the American Society of Landscape Architects with the Olmsted brothers, Beatrix Jones Farrand and seven others in 1899. Out of his office in New York City, he prepared university master plans and designed urban parks. His planning aesthetic was aligned with the City Beautiful movement.

15 - There were no new buildings constructed at Mount Hermon between 1915 and 1952 and only three at Northfield.

16 - *Circle in Time,* page 80.

17 - *Lift Thine Eyes*, page 135.

18 - *Circle in Time*, page 126

19 - *Hotchkiss the Place*, page 31.

20 - *Lift Thine Eyes,* page 201.

21 - Linda Tischler, *Fast Company,* "Prep schools lead the way on sustainable living" November 2011.

22 - Choate Rosemary Hall and Deerfield Academy are arch rivals in athletic competition since "Deerfield Day"—or Choate Rosemary Hall Day, depending which side of the ball you are on—was first organized in autumn 1922.

The Lawrenceville School
The Bowl

7: THE WHOLE CAMPUS: PHYSICAL AND FINANCIAL PLANNING

Place is a powerful thing. . . . It is an art form that reflects the values and vision of its founder and the social, political, and economic landscape of its time.

Sally Atwood Hamilton, Northfield Mount Hermon, Class of 1965[1]

Formation of the whole student, as developed in the previous four chapters, requires a supportive environment. When a school's aspirations to nurture the whole student and create a whole campus are aligned, the power of place becomes palpable. Campus planners, architects, and other design professionals, together with their client, create this sense of place.

The first comprehensive campus plans for colleges and college preparatory boarding schools were produced in the late 1800s. In earlier years, campuses developed incrementally. Development was limited by available funds and most buildings were located to meet short-term needs. Planning, as a discipline and profession, grew out of existing disciplines such as land surveying and civil, water, and sanitary engineering. Over time, campus planners began collaborating with architects and engaging with emerging disciplines such as landscape architecture, transportation planning, and way-finding (graphic design) to form teams able to produce comprehensive plans. Master plans, however, were often abandoned or modified radically as immediate needs or changing goals superseded the vision of the long-range plan. Today, integrated campus plans—combining academic, financial, and physical planning—are usually preceded by a strategic planning process that articulates in detail the school's mission and vision of the future. A "framework" plan is then developed with several "horizons," becoming less specific as the horizon recedes. Regular updates keep the framework relevant. The adage "not everything planned is built, and not everything built is planned" recognizes the inherent dilemma in predicting and controlling future campus development.

The rise of campus planning was followed by the advent of major fund raising campaigns.[2] Prior to these campaigns, private schools relied on a combination of bequests, individual one-off donations, state support, borrowing, and tuition to fund their operations and physical plant. In the early twentieth century, public funds became unavailable and operating expenses began to outpace tuition. Bequests were unpredictable and, in many cases, restricted. Rather than solicit one gift at a time, schools embarked on multi-year fund raising campaigns. They formed alumni associations and development offices to maintain ties with graduates, some of whom were heirs to large estates and others who earned fortunes in business. Today, when schools identify a need for capital improvements, they often commission a campus plan before launching a campaign. In addition to soliciting gifts for proposed new and renovated buildings and grounds, campaigns usually include an appeal for donations to increase

Yale University
Brick Row
c. 1807

the school's endowment. Earnings from endowment investments support student scholarships, faculty salaries, and operating costs.

As campuses expanded, certain planning strategies were successful enough that they became models for other campuses. Yale College, for example, built a succession of alternating "chapels"—classroom and assembly uses—and dormitories from 1752 to 1835, known as the "brick row." Yale aligned the buildings parallel to the street and to the west edge of the New Haven Green.[3] The Andover Theological Seminary adopted this strategy in the 1820s to build "seminary row", set back from the street by an expansive lawn. Thomas Jefferson's design for the University of Virginia's "academical village" in the 1820s featured symmetrically aligned ranges of classroom buildings and living quarters on either side of "the Lawn" with the Rotunda (library) centered at one end. Delano and Aldrich adapted Jefferson's axial plan for "the Bowl" at The Lawrenceville School in the 1930s, a strategy they also employed at the Yale Divinity School about the same time. Noyes Circle, laid out with a 500-foot diameter in 1864 at Vassar College, was originally used for exercise and gardening. A segment of the circle now forms the footprint of a dormitory designed by Eero Saarinen. Frederick Law Olmsted's plan for Lawrenceville in the 1880's uses an irregular circle to organize student "houses" and other buildings in an arboretum setting. The seventeenth-century settlers of the New Haven Colony laid out their town in a nine-square plan with the center square as a common green space. The Choate Rosemary Hall campus was developed in the early twentieth century within a four-square grid determined by two pre-existing cross streets. Today, each quadrant has a predominant use: student life, dormitories, academic, and athletic. At the University

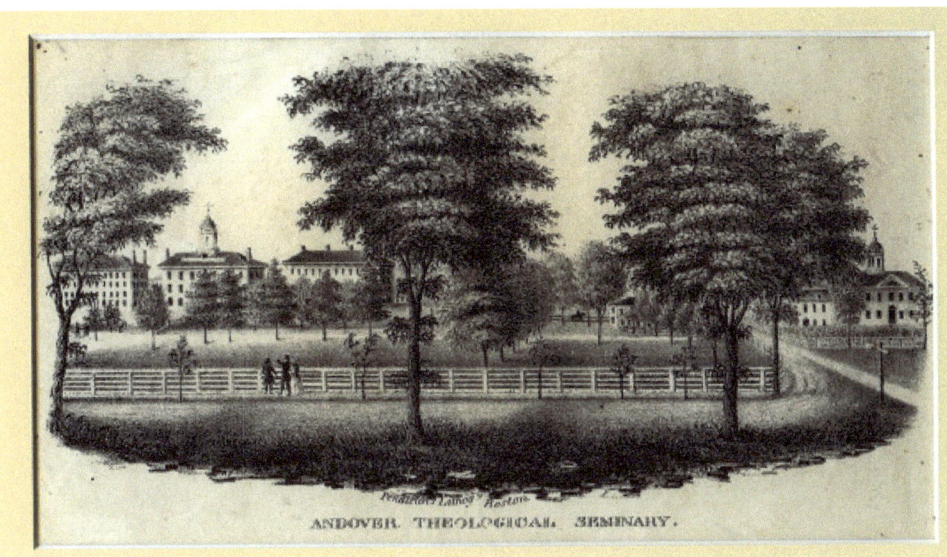

Phillips Academy
Andover
Seminary Row
c. 1830

of Pennsylvania, Woodlawn Avenue—originally a thoroughfare, now a pedestrian walk—intersects the orthogonal urban grid at a forty-five degree angle. This diagonal creates unique building sites, open spaces, and short cuts for pedestrians. In Choate Rosemary Hall's academic quadrant, site plans for the arts center and the mathematics and computer science building enable diagonal movement from the perimeter to buildings deeper in the quadrant. Princeton University's early twentieth century dormitory quadrangle on the southwest corner of campus is open on one side to allow views of the upper campus. The four-dormitory complex, designed by Charles Z. Klauder[4] at St. Paul's School in the 1920s, is also a quadrangle open on one side to views of the stream and meadow. At Wellesley College near Boston, building location and orientation are determined by hills and valleys, reinforced by groves of trees and a lake. The Mount Hermon campus and the former Northfield campus follow a similar naturalistic approach. Very few campus plans, even as initially envisioned, are pure examples of one or another of these typologies. Hybrids, evident in the following sections on campus planning at Andover and Hotchkiss, are more common.

CAMPUS PLANNING AT PHILLIPS ACADEMY ANDOVER

Phillips Academy Andover is situated on Academy Hill in Andover, Massachusetts. Located on the Merrimack River some twenty miles north of Boston, Andover was first settled in 1636. By 1790, shortly before the academy was founded, the town's population was about 3,000. Main Street—the spine of the early settlement—bisects the town and the academy campus. The current school is an amalgam of four institutions:

THE WHOLE CAMPUS: PHYSICAL AND FINANCIAL PLANNING

Phillips Academy
Andover
Model of the Ideal
1928

Phillips Academy
Andover
The Vista
1932

Phillips Academy (founded in 1797), Andover Theological Seminary (founded in 1808), Abbot Female Academy (founded in 1828), and the Andover English Academy and Teacher's Seminary (founded 1827, closed in 1847). According to an observer, in 1865, Phillips Academy had "no discernible campus."⁵ This observation was likely based on the absence of dormitories and a chapel, as student housing and communal worship were integrated within the town. The Theological Seminary, by comparison, had a robust campus, featuring a row of three stately brick buildings—built between 1809 and 1821—on the east side of the town's Main Street. A walkway lined on both sides by elm trees—later named Elm Arch—and a row of elaborate faculty houses completed the seminary's campus.

In 1889, the academy's trustees formed a Committee on Real Estate and Buildings to oversee campus development. Two years later, the committee hired Frederick Law Olmsted to prepare a plan for its land on the west side of Main Street. Olmsted and his successor firm, Olmsted Brothers, advised the trustees from that initial commission until 1965. Olmsted prepared two plans, one in 1891 and another in 1903. The first plan interspersed ten small recitation buildings and nine cottage style dormitories along two gently curving roads west of the seminary's faculty houses. Andover built four of the cottages and one larger dormitory in the 1890s. The second plan, influenced by Beaux-Arts design principles and a shift from the earlier domestic scale of the campus to a more collegiate one, was axial and quadrangular. The 1903 plan proposed a new main academy building, several classroom buildings, several large dormitories, an infirmary, and a library. The school built four dormitories and the infirmary, designed by Guy Lowell,[6] between 1911 and 1913.

While Olmsted's plan and Lowell's buildings were progressing, the Theological Seminary decided to move from Andover to Cambridge, Massachusetts. The academy purchased the seminary's land and buildings, precipitating a heated debate about where to focus campus expansion: east or west of Main Street. After World War I, influential trustees George Case and Thomas Cochran successfully argued that the former seminary row was the logical center for an expanded academy campus. They hired Charles A. Platt,[7] a distinguished Boston architect to re-envision the campus on the east side of Main Street. Together with Cochran—who had been made chairman of the trustee's building and grounds committee—and Charles Sawyer—the school's treasurer and adviser to Principal Alfred Stearns—Platt embarked on an ambitious plan known as The Idealized Andover[8]. Platt's description of the working relationship among the three men was "a notable triumvirate." The trustees concurrently launched a $1.5 million capital campaign to implement the plan.

Platt's first move in 1922 was to relocate Pearson Hall, the middle building of seminary row, in order to open a vista from the proposed new academy building westward toward

The Circle:
Abbott Female Academy

the hills.[9] By 1932, Guy Lowell and Platt had designed ten major buildings in the Colonial Revival style. More buildings were moved, and some demolished—particularly the seminary's High Victorian Gothic Stone Chapel and Brechin Hall—to create quadrangles and sites for prominent buildings including an art gallery, library, and chapel. Lowell successfully argued that quadrangles should have open corners, rather than be completely enclosed, in order to frame vistas and allow diagonal movement. Following the deaths of Lowell, Platt, and Cochran, Andover hired Perry, Shaw & Hepburn, the Boston based firm that had designed Colonial Williamsburg, to continue the triumvirate's work. By 1937, despite the economic hardships of the Great Depression, the academy had built nine additional buildings, including an expansion of faculty row.

After World War II, Modernism replaced Colonial Revival as the preferred style for planning and building at Andover and elsewhere. To achieve this transition, the academy hired The Architects Collaborative (TAC), founded by Walter Gropius—the former Bauhaus director and then current Dean of the Harvard Graduate

School of Design—as campus planner and architect. Between 1957 and 1966, TAC planned and designed an ensemble of five dormitories in a natural setting between Rabbit Pond and the Moncrieff Cochran bird sanctuary. On the central campus they designed a visual arts center as an infill building between the Platt-designed art gallery and administration building. Floor-to-ceiling windows on the campus side and a ground level walkway through the building visually and physically connect the building to its environs. In 1963, to accommodate a flexible laboratory concept of teaching science, TAC designed a one-story open plan laboratory building. Because this teaching method proved problematic, the academy demolished the building and in 2004 built a new three-story science building on an adjacent lot.

The advent of coeducation in the early 1970s presented the academy with another opportunity: acquisition of the nearby Abbot Female Academy campus. Once the two schools had merged, the Abbot females joined the Andover males in Academy Hill's dormitories, classrooms, and playing fields. The three–building core of the Abbot campus, arrayed on the perimeter of a circular drive, was built between 1829 and 1903. The earlier buildings were designed in the Greek Revival style and the later ones in Romanesque Revival and Renaissance Revival styles. To fully realize an 1886 master plan by Hartwell and Richardson, three of the older buildings were moved, two new ones built, and one demolished. The buildings are currently used by the academy for administration, faculty housing, and community services.

Andover's commitment to campus development on the east side of Main Street has both positive and negative effects. The campus planned and built during the 1920s and 1930s using the former seminary buildings as a starting point is stylistically cohesive. The courtyards known as the Great Quad and the more intimate Flagstaff Quad are places to linger and remember. The Great Lawn facing Main Street and the western part of the campus provides a green foreground to the buildings along Elm Arch. The Vista not only provides views of the western mountains, but when approached from the west, proceeds on-axis with the elevated Samuel Phillips Hall. The remaining buildings on the west side of Main Street, however, have been somewhat orphaned by the strong commitment to the east campus. The self-contained, six-dormitory quadrangle on the south side could be mistaken for a different school. The three remaining cottages are left-overs from the time of the first Olmsted plan. The Peabody Museum, although fronting on Main Street, is isolated among a row of private houses. The former Abbott campus was intentionally set apart from the seminary and academy and remains apart.

In comparison, the campus of Williams College in Williamstown, Massachusetts, likewise bisected by the town's Main Street, is balanced. Larger buildings—science, athletics, and museum—are located on the south side of Main Street, while the north side contains the library, student center, and performing and visual arts. Student housing, dining, and classroom buildings are distributed on both sides of Main Street.

CAMPUS PLANNING AT THE HOTCHKISS SCHOOL

The Hotchkiss School, like Andover, experienced a succession of campus plans and capital campaigns. The campus is located in northwestern Connecticut on the banks of Lake Wonoscopomuc in the Salisbury Mountains. The school's founder, Mary Bissell Hotchkiss, donated sixty-five acres for the first campus in 1891. Over

The Hotchkiss School
Aerial Rendering
c1892

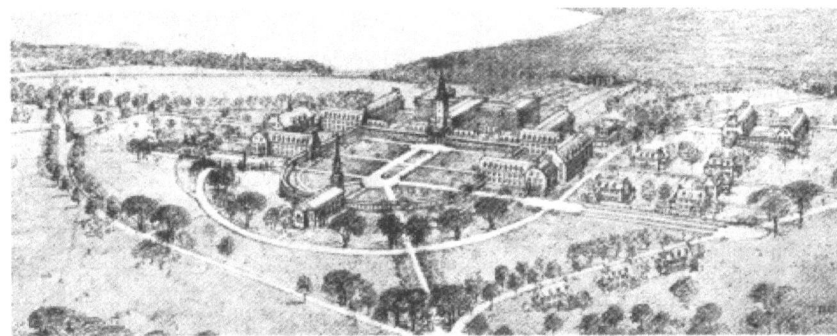

The Hotchkiss School,
Cass Gilbert Plan
1915 and 1925

time, the school acquired additional farmland and woodland, to create the current 827-acre campus. Much of this land is protected from development, maintaining the site's rural character and providing a buffer from potential incompatible uses.

The most striking feature of the built environment at Hotchkiss is the multi-purpose megastructure simply known as Main. Designed by Bruce Price,[10] the original Main building housed all the functions of the school, emulating eighteenth-century Nassau Hall at Princeton and University Hall at Brown. A straight three-hundred foot long corridor linked ground floor classrooms on the west end, offices for administration and faculty and a meeting room in the center, and a chapel, dining hall, and gym on the east. The central block had two upper stories of student rooms. The first graduating class consisted of fourteen members, but a year later when enrollment was boosted to one hundred students, a free-standing dorm, Bissell Hall, was built. Main exists today but only after many renovations, partial demolitions, and additions over the past one-hundred-twenty-five years. In 1906, the school hired Ernest Bowditch, a civil engineer and landscape architect, to plan the grounds. Bowditch, who served for twelve years, established a tree nursery and plant greenhouse. During his tenure, a nine-hole golf course encircling the campus was laid out.

In 1915, the trustees commissioned Cass

The Hotchkiss School
Aerial view looking
northwest
c. 1970

The Hotchkiss School
Master Plan 2001
Main Bulding
First Floor

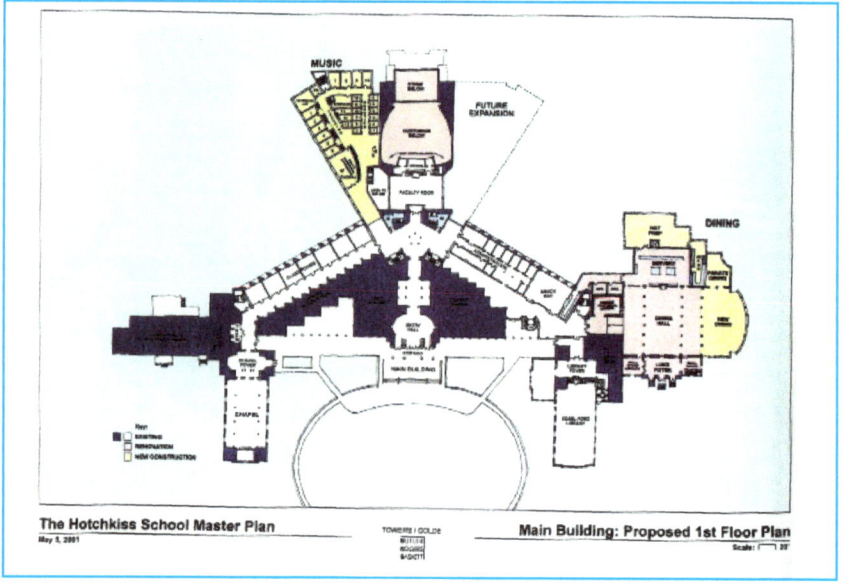

Gilbert,[11] an architect trained at the École des Beaux-Arts in Paris, to prepare a master plan for an expanded campus to support enrollment of 288 students. After the end of World War I, they launched a $2.5 million fund raising campaign to implement the planned expansion and to fund an endowment for scholarships and faculty salaries. The centerpiece of Gilbert's 1925 revised plan was a memorial tower—honoring Hotchkiss men who died in the war—surmounting a new main academic building. He planned this tower on axis with a proposed new chapel and

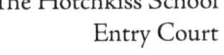
The Hotchkiss School
Entry Court

steeple, connected by a wide mall flanked by new dormitories. After completing two dormitories that established the "Hotchkiss Georgian" style, Gilbert resigned in a dispute over proposed departures from his plan. Ironically, in 1937, the state re-routed a portion of Route 112 that would have made his plan feasible. The trustees replaced Gilbert with another New York firm, Delano & Aldrich,[12] who scaled down Gilbert's ambitious plan. They designed two additional dormitories and a chapel before the onset of the Great Depression and World War II.

In 1945, the trustees launched another campaign targeting $1.5 million for a library, an indoor swimming pool, a new dining room and kitchen, and additions and renovations to Main. The campaign's success enabled construction of all the buildings. Delano & Aldrich, as Gilbert before them, had proposed replacing Main without success. In 1967, the seventy-fifth anniversary of the school's founding gave new impetus to this proposal.

Anticipating alumni pride in this milestone, the trustees embarked on an ambitious five-year capital campaign with a goal of $8.95 million. The program called for replacing the original sections of Main with a contemporary building, a free-standing science building, and two new dormitories on the west side of campus. An alumnus, T. Merrill Prentice, the architect chosen for the science building, and Paul Rudolph,[13] who had been hired to design the dormitories, vied for the prize of designing the new Main. The trustees, however, selected Hugh Stubbins,[14] who had recently completed the initial buildings on the campus of the newly opened Hampshire College, and several buildings at Harvard and Princeton. His plan was brilliant—retaining the spirit of the original while taking better advantage of the sloping site and views of the lake—but the "brutal" character of the building's exterior, particularly the entrance, seemed

Phillips Exeter Academy

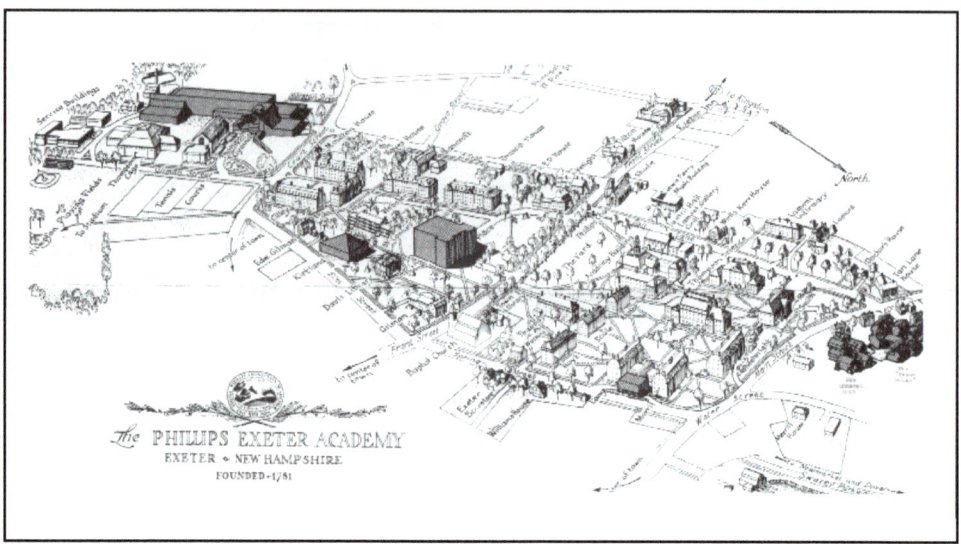

out of place at Hotchkiss. Two later attempts to mitigate the effect, one by opening up the blank brick blocks with glass, and another by superimposing an over-scaled triumphal arched portico, were also problematic.

In 2001, the trustees undertook another ambitious building program and capital campaign. Butler Rogers Baskett (BRB)[15] produced a master plan that included a music wing addition to Main, a new dormitory, renovation of the 1920s era dormitories, a dining hall addition and renovation, a reconstituted athletic center, and renovation of several non-academic buildings. Significantly, about $2.7 million was allocated to landscape improvements. BRB's team included Towers/Golde, the first landscape firm to comprehensively plan the campus grounds since Ernest Bowditch did almost a century earlier.

The school's long-term commitment to the concept of concentrating academic and social functions in one main building and distributing free-standing dormitories across campus has been successful. There are limits, however, to how many additions the main building can sustain. One is available land and the other is coherence. The central campus, bordered by two state roads and the lake, is also ringed by a nine-hole golf course. The open space between the north end of the main building and the lake, is the fairway of the fourth and fifth holes. While this land use is unusual, golf seems to be part of the school's DNA. The strength of the main building is its mixed-use quality, but after so many renovations and additions, it begins to resemble a hospital complex in terms of way-finding and legibility.

Hotchkiss, like Choate Rosemary Hall, is a leader in environmental science. While Choate Rosemary Hall's focus is on wise energy consumption, Hotchkiss emphasizes wise energy production. The Woodchip Central Heating Facility, built in 2012, is exemplary in its use of biomass fuel—wood chips from sustainably managed regional forests—that reduces CO_2 emissions compared with non-renewable energy sources. Each of the Eight Schools offer courses in environmental science. Hotchkiss offered the first Advanced Placement course in the subject while Choate Rosemary Hall offers and environmental immersion program. As environmental science is an emerging field, the schools can benefit from collaboration with each other and the colleges that graduates may attend.

MANAGING THE FINANCIAL CRISES OF THE 1970S: PHILLIPS EXETER ACADEMY

The perfect financial storm of the 1970s—the rising cost of energy and other operating expenses, financial market losses, and double-digit inflation—battered all Eight Schools and many others. Exeter, having a reputation as the school with the deepest pockets, provides a cautionary tale.

Prior to the onset of this inflationary recession, the Exeter trustees had launched a fundraising campaign, The Long Step Forward, targeting $13 million for buildings and $8 million for endowment. Proposed buildings included a new gym, two new dormitories, and a dining hall addition. A new library, dining hall, and theater were also built in the early 1970s. When construction costs escalated and anticipated gifts failed to materialize, the trustees extended the campaign and the goal. In order to keep up with expenses, they increased tuition, borrowed money, and resorted to tapping endowment principal. By 1979, a combination of investment losses, debt service, and inflation had reduced Exeter's purchasing power by almost fifty percent.[16]

During this time, remarkably, Exeter admitted its first class of girls. The academy's goal was to achieve parity—equal numbers of male and female students—without reducing the number of male students. While additional tuition was welcome, the demand on faculty and facilities introduced another challenge. In 1978, around the two-hundredth anniversary of the academy's founding, the trustees launched a $22.6 million campaign, primarily to restore and grow the endowment. In addition, by restructuring the operating budget, creating reserves for unexpected expenses, outsourcing endowment investment management, stipulating an annual spend rate,[17] enhancing the annual alumni giving program, and other reforms, Exeter was able to balance its budget and preserve its endowment. Now, forty years later, the academy's pockets are deeper than ever.

SUMMARY

An effective campus plan is usually based on numbers: students, faculty, acres of land, square footage of buildings, and endowment valuation; and ratios: students/teacher, male/female students, square feet/student, and endowment/student. School websites often have virtual tours for prospective students and profiles of current students. None of these data or online visuals, however, can fully convey the experience of being on campus. Campus planners and architects strive to create a place that is indeed a "powerful thing." The next chapter focuses on the architects' contribution.

Notes

1 - *Lift Thine Eyes*, preface ix.

2 - Schools began organized capital campaigns in the 1920s. Deerfield, for example, conducted seven major campaigns between 1929 and 1988. Bruce Barton, advertising executive, author, trustee, and childhood friend of the headmaster Frank Boyden, led five of these campaigns, raising over $9 million for twelve buildings. A dormitory was dedicated in his name in 1962.

3 - Yale demolished eight of the nine "brick row" buildings between 1869 and 1901 to build a continuous wall of masonry dormitories fronting the Green, penetrated only by an arched, gated, passageway.

4 - Charles Klauder (active 1900s–1930s). Klauder practiced from his office in Philadelphia, originally with a partner Frank Miles Day. His firm designed many Gothic Revival (Collegiate Gothic) dormitories at Princeton in the 1910s and later at St. Paul's School. His book *College Architecture in America* was a practical, "how-to," guide for planners and architects.

5 - *The Campus Guide: Phillips Academy Andover,* page 2.

6 - Guy Lowell. See Chapter 5, note 21. Lowell had presided over campus planning and building design at Andover for over 26 years before he died in 1927.

7 - Charles Platt. See Chapter 2, note 20.

8 - Olmsted Brothers had built an enormous model of the campus, but by this time Platt had superseded the Olmsted firm as the chief campus planner.

9 - Tucker House, a former seminary faculty house on the west side of Main Street, designed in the Queen Anne style, was also moved so as not to impinge on the vista.

10 - Bruce Price (active 1870s–1900s) from his office in New York City, Price designed Shingle Style houses in Tuxedo Park, NY, Romanesque revival dormitories at Yale and Teacher's College at Columbia, a Georgian revival mansion for Jay Gould in New Jersey, and the Chateau Frontenac in Quebec.

11 - Cass Gilbert. See Chapter 3, note 15

12 - Delano & Aldrich. See Chapter 2, note 24.

13 - Paul Rudolph (active 1940s–1990s). Early in his career Rudolph designed single family houses in his native Florida and toward the end of his career, high rise buildings in southeast Asia. During the 1960s, Rudolph was dean of the Department of Architecture at Yale when he designed the studio building for the School of Art and Architecture. As Rudolph was known for his design of megastructures, one wonders why he did not receive the commission for the Hotchkiss Main Building.

14 - Hugh Stubbins (active 1960s–1990s) designed the first academic and student life buildings at Hampshire College, part of the Five College Consortium, in Amherst, MA. The campus opened in 1970 around the same time Stubbin's Main Building at Hotchkiss opened. His portfolio includes academic buildings at Harvard and Princeton, a presidential library, and several urban high-rise office buildings.

15 - Butler Rogers Baskett, aka BRB Architects (active 1980s–present). BRB's practice, headquartered in New York City, includes a large portfolio of buildings for college and universities and private independent schools in the northeast. For Hotchkiss, they partnered with landscape architects Towers/Golde.

16 - *After the Harkness Gift* page 223–24.

17 - A spend rate limits the percentage of endowment income allocated to the operating budget in a given year.

THE WHOLE CAMPUS: PHYSICAL AND FINANCIAL PLANNING

Phillips Academy Andover
Main School Building

8: ART AND ARCHITECTURE

All these (public and private buildings) must be built with due reference to durability, convenience, and beauty.

Vitruvius, *The Ten Books on Architecture* Twentieth-century translation[1]

Two-thousand years after Vitruvius codified the essential criteria that all buildings must meet, his code is still valid. Durability, also translated firmness, is essential if a building is to survive the vicissitudes of floods, gale force winds, fires, earthquakes, explosions, environmental hazards, or other destructive forces. Convenience, also translated commodity, is a measure of how well the design of a building suits its purpose. When needs change, a building must adapt to survive. Beauty, also translated delight, leaves a favorable, lasting impression on those who experience the intangible, intrinsic character of a building or landscape. Buildings are vulnerable to changing perception of beauty, which, as we know, is in the eye of the beholder. A truly successful building, for example Bulfinch Hall[2] at Phillips Academy Andover, satisfies all three criteria.

Designed in 1818 by Asher Benjamin—who also designed Deerfield Academy's first school building in 1798—Bulfinch Hall was Andover's second purpose-built academic building. There were three classrooms and a library on the first floor and an open second floor used for assemblies and recitations. Benjamin designed the exterior walls using brick in an attempt to avoid the fate of the first, a wooden academy building that had been destroyed by fire a year earlier. The building was re-purposed as a gymnasium in 1867 when a larger main academy building opened. In 1896, however, the structure was gutted by fire, leaving only the exterior walls standing. The floors, roof, interior partitions, and finishes were combustible, characteristic of most masonry bearing wall buildings of the time. In 1902, it was resurrected as a dining commons. Guy Lowell designed the interior with a dining room on the first floor, a larger banquet hall on the second, and an addition in the rear that served as the kitchen. When the academy, then under the influence of the architect Charles Platt, opened a new larger, more elaborate, dining commons in 1936, Bulfinch Hall was ready for another makeover. Perry, Shaw & Hepburn, the architects for Colonial Williamsburg, renovated the interior for use by the English Department and added a cupola and pediment on the street facade.

Bulfinch Hall remains on its original site, but Andover was not reluctant to move a building if it interfered with some higher priority. Four buildings, including the middle seminary building were moved to open up Platt's east-west Vista. Another two buildings were moved to create sites, one for the chapel and the other

Phillips Academy Andover
Bulfinch Hall

for an archaeology museum. Two "leftover" seminary buildings built in the mid-nineteenth century were demolished around 1930 because of "their objectionable Gothic styling and because their locations 'destroyed the balance' that Platt was creating."[3] At Choate, during the tenure of headmaster George St. John (1908-47), about twenty houses were moved to the periphery from the main street that bisected the campus to make the campus "look less like a residential neighborhood and more like an academic institution."[4]

ARCHITECTURAL STYLE

For Choate's headmaster, his architects, and heads of other schools, the salient question was: what, exactly, does an academic institution look like? The appearance and identity of a school depends largely on the architectural style of its buildings. Style is determined by several factors, including: time and place—a fifteenth-century building in Florence, Italy compared with a seventeenth-century building in the North American colonies; cultural and historical associations—a royal palace compared with a town meeting hall; construction technology and materials—a single-story, timber-framed building compared with a high-rise, steel-framed tower; organization of floor plans, composition of exterior elevations, and massing of volumes—rational and formal compared with romantic and multi-faceted; and, most subjective of all, "taste." To identify a particular style is complicated by the reality that there are very few examples of an ideologically pure style. Most buildings are pragmatic hybrids. Furthermore, classifications such as classical, modern, or Victorian are too broad to be very meaningful, and the nomenclature is often contradictory. One person's Georgian may be another person's Neoclassical.[5]

For most of the eighteenth and nineteenth centuries, American architects, like their European counterparts, designed within the architectural tradition broadly known as Classicism. This tradition is derived from ancient civilizations of Greece and the Rome, although it has evolved in many ways over the past 2500 years. The Renaissance—fifteenth and sixteenth centuries—was the first revival of classical architecture since antiquity. Spearheaded by the Florentine architect Filippo Brunelleschi at the beginning of the fifteenth century, the movement spread throughout Europe over the subsequent two centuries. It was adopted by architects like Andrea Palladio in northern Italy and Inigo Jones in England.[6] Baroque design, a seventeenth-century elaboration of the Renaissance canon, was practiced by architects such as Christopher Wren in England and by Francesco Borromini in Italy. In the eighteenth century, architects began to reject what they saw as the excesses of Baroque style and reverted to a purer form of classicism, inspired

Historic Deerfield
Wells-Thorn House

Historic Deerfield
Barnard House

by the earlier Italian Renaissance and informed by new archaeological excavations of ancient Roman sites. Palladian architecture, popularized by James Gibbs in eighteenth-century England, enjoyed its own revival during the reigns of King George I, II, and III (1714–1820). The tail end of Wren's Baroque, along with Gibbs' subsequent revival of Palladian architecture, became known as Georgian in colonial America. The following is a brief primer on architectural styles as they apply to buildings of the Eight Schools.

BUILDING IN COLONIAL NEW ENGLAND

The first colonists in New England survived by building primitive dugouts and so-called "English wigwams" for shelter, and blockhouses and palisades for defense. Some seventeenth-century colonists were skilled in medieval timber framing and owned tools adequate for cutting, shaping, and joining wood posts, girts, and purlins. They used clapboard sheathing for exterior walls and wood shingles for roofs. In 1684, for members of the Pennsylvania colony, William Penn published a practical building guide for timber construction, including how to forge iron nails. As the colonies matured in the eighteenth century, colonial builders and designers became aware of architectural developments in England, developing their own variant of the Georgian style. By 1724, for example, Philadelphia tradesmen had formed the Carpenters' Company to codify building methods and to introduce "the canons of eighteenth-century classicism as these were set forth in the standard English treatises of the early part of the century."[7] The town of Deerfield, Massachusetts, although far removed from the eighteenth century cultural capitals of Philadelphia and Boston, has a trove of colonial architecture. The design of these buildings generally followed Georgian precedents, although they were constructed of wood and displayed limited carved wood ornament. Due to preservation efforts by Historic Deerfield and Deerfield

ART AND ARCHITECTURE

Northfield Mount
Hermon School
Auditorium

St. Paul's School
Chapel of St. Peter and
St. Paul

Academy—one of the Eight Schools founded in the late eighteenth century—some of these buildings function today as dormitories, faculty houses, offices, and house museums.

NINETEENTH-CENTURY REVIVAL STYLES

A variety of picturesque revival styles characterize nineteenth-century American architecture. In the 1810's, Greek Revival became the preferred style for government buildings, banks,

Northfield Mount
Hermon School
Sage Chapel
Interior 1909

courthouses, and manor houses. The nation's capitol, inspired by the symbol of Greek democracy, provided the model: freestanding, generally fluted, columns with bases and capitals of the Greek orders, generally Ionic; pediments with cornices supported by dentils; sloped tiled roofs; and light colored, dressed stone laid in ashlar.[8] Where stone was unavailable or unaffordable, builders used wood, painted white, to resemble marble. The few remaining examples of this style at the Eight Schools are wooden houses that were moved to the campus periphery.

By mid-century, the trend shifted to the Italianate style, later known as Italian Renaissance Revival. Inspired by the architecture of Tuscany, this style is characterized by cubic massing, off-center towers, low-pitch, hipped roofs, deep eaves supported by brackets, tall chimneys, semicircular arched openings, balconies, and ornamental ironwork. Although few examples exist on Eight Schools' campuses, an extraordinary one is the Auditorium Building on the former Northfield campus.

Gothic Revival, which flourished in England between 1830 and 1870, arrived in the eastern United States in the 1860s. Gothic architecture—originally developed by European cathedral builders in the twelfth-to-fifteenth centuries—is characterized by pointed arches, ribbed vaults, external buttresses, and strong vertical proportions. The Chapel of St. Peter and St. Paul is an outstanding example of Gothic Revival on a campus of the Eight Schools.[9] At Northfield, Shepley, Rutan and Coolidge designed the Russell Sage chapel in a Gothic Revival style using Rockport granite for the exterior walls and framing the sanctuary roof with tie-beam, queen-post trusses.

High Victorian Gothic is characterized by a multitude of multi-colored materials—several types of stone, brick laid in patterns, glazed tile, and terra cotta ornament—asymmetrical massing

ART AND ARCHITECTURE

Northfield Mount Hermon
Marquand Hall

Northfield Mount Hermon
Betsey Moody Infirmary

often with conical towers and oriel windows, and steep, often polychromatic, slate roofs. Marquand Hall on the former Northfield campus, designed by Rand and Taylor in 1884, is an example of this style. Many High Victorian buildings were considered "ugly" and demolished by succeeding generations. Brechin Hall, for example, was built in 1866 for the Andover Theological Seminary in a Venetian Gothic style. When the academy bought the seminary and Charles Platt remade the campus in the 1930s, Brechin Hall, and another building of the same era and style, were demolished simply "because they did not fit into the colonial revival campus."[10] Romanesque Revival is uniquely American, popularized by H.H. Richardson[11] who practiced in Boston in the late-nineteenth century. The style is characterized by rough cut stone masonry, semicircular arches, turrets, towers, terra cotta trim, steep slate roofs, and relatively small, deep-set window openings. Memorial Hall on the Circle at The Lawrenceville School—designed by Peabody & Stearns in 1884—is an example of this style.

The Queen Anne style—actually a revival style as it was loosely based on vernacular English domestic architecture during the reign of Queen Anne (1702–1714)—was developed by the English architect Richard Norman Shaw in the early 1870s.[12] Robert Peabody, in his 1877 "A Talk about Queen Anne," argued that the style was a clean break from Gothic Revival and a return to American colonial building before the advent of refined European styles in the early nineteenth century.[13] The Circle houses on the Lawrenceville campus demonstrate Peabody's version of the style in brick with wood trim. On the former Northfield campus several wood framed Queen Anne houses were built, including the Betsey Moody Infirmary.

In the late nineteenth century, American architectural students such as Richard Morris

Lawrenceville School
Memorial Hall Entrance

ENTRANCE TO MEMORIAL HALL

Hunt and Cass Gilbert enrolled in the French École des Beaux-Arts. The École celebrated Renaissance planning and design principles such as hierarchy of spaces, bilateral symmetry, axial vistas and focal points, and highly elaborated sculptural exteriors. Mid-to-late nineteenth-century exhibitions and world fairs in London, Paris, and Chicago popularized the Beaux-Arts style and influenced American city planning and monumental architecture for decades. Thompson Gymnasium, designed by Ralph Adams Cram in 1918, is a rare example of this style on an Eight Schools campus. Others include a library, dormitory, and gym by Parish and Schroeder on the Mount Hermon campus around 1910.

As a footnote to this history of revival styles, Frank Lloyd Wright—perhaps the one American architect with whom a layperson might be familiar—was sidelined by these rear-guard movements. In 1940, Wright said "They killed Sullivan and they nearly killed me," 'they' being the revival style practitioners and Sullivan being Wright's mentor in Chicago.[14] Perhaps that explains why Wright never received a commission to design a building for any of the Eight Schools, which thrived on revival styles during his career (1890s to 1950s).

THE TWENTIETH CENTURY
GEORGIAN AND COLONIAL REVIVAL 1910s THROUGH 1930s

In the first three decades of the twentieth century, Modernism—as practiced in Europe most notably by Walter Gropius, Le Corbusier, and Mies van der Rohe—was beginning to influence the course of American architectural design. With several notable exceptions, however, mainstream American architects concealed advanced structural systems behind revival style facades.[15] The

Phillips Academy
Andover
Samuel Phillips Hall

Phillips Exeter Academy
Webster and
Dunbar Halls

architects favored by the Eight Schools looked to eighteenth-century English precedents for inspiration and meaning. Hotchkiss, founded in 1892, and Choate, founded in 1896, soon established their preference for Georgian architecture. All of Choate's new buildings until the 1950s, and all Hotchkiss' dormitory buildings from the 1920s through the 1930s, were designed in some version of the Georgian Revival style. According to Peter Pennoyer, an architect, author and historic preservationist, the Hotchkiss "style evoked by (Cass) Gilbert is the Neo-Classical branch of the Georgian Revival."[16] The temple-front-and-spire formula—derived from Christopher Wren's Baroque and James Gibb's Palladian designs during the reign of King George II—was the source for

Choate Rosemary Hall
Mellon Humanities Center

Exeter's Fourth Academy Building, designed by Ralph Adams Cram in 1915, and Andover's Samuel Phillips Hall, designed in 1924 by Guy Lowell.

Colonial Williamsburg, Virginia, was another major influence on the evolution of this style in America, and in particular at the Eight Schools. The exceptions are St. Paul's, which transitioned from Gothic Revival to Collegiate Gothic in this period[17] and Mount Hermon, which needed no new buildings between 1915 and 1952. The reconstruction and reproduction of Williamsburg in the 1930s, guided by Perry Shaw and Hepburn, gave rise to the term "Colonial Revival." The substitution of "Colonial" for "Georgian" is significant, in that it connotes patriotism but insignificant stylistically, in that the terms are often used interchangeably. The Georgian aspect of Colonial emulated by the architects of the 1920s and 1930s was precisely the Colonial that the Queen Anne architects had rejected.[18]

Harvard University's River Houses—dormitory quadrangles built from 1913 through 1930—became the gold standard for Georgian Revival campus architecture. The common characteristics as they apply to the Eight Schools include: a stone base, red brick walls, pitched slate roofs, gable ends in the form of a pediment, attic dormers, eaves supported by dentils, brick chimneys, an occasional tiered tower with cupola, double-hung, mullioned windows, an occasional Palladian window, entryways with porticos, wood columns with carved wood capitals and bases, white-painted wood trim, and occasional marble trim. Building footprints are usually rectangular with an optional projected central bay, end bays, and an occasional ell. Massing is usually two-to-three stories with basement and attic. This formula served academic, dormitory, and athletic buildings during this period.

Variations are abundant. The Mellon Humanities Center—built in 1938 as the Paul Mellon Science Hall at Choate Rosemary

The Lawrenceville School
McKenzie Administration
Building

The Lawrenceville School
Father's (Pop) Hall

Hall—has a tall hipped roof surmounted by a wood balustrade, evocative of the southern adaption of the Colonial Revival style. At The Lawrenceville School, Delano and Aldrich adapted the segmented dome and columned portico of Thomas Jefferson's Monticello for the McKenzie Administration building. Modification of the temple-front-and-spire composition—where the freestanding columns are flattened into pilasters between arched openings and the portico is recessed into the building volume—can be found at Andover's Cochran Chapel by Charles Platt and Delano and Aldrich's Father's (Pop) Hall at Lawrenceville.

Georgian Revival, however, increasingly became an empty vessel. Rapid advances in science and technology in the first half of the twentieth century inspired a new machine age

Phillips Exeter Academy Class of 1945 Library

aesthetic. European architects, who had developed this new aesthetic, emigrated to the United States in the 1930s and influenced generations of American architects.[19]

MODERNIST ARCHITECTURE 1950s TO THE PRESENT

The seeds of modern architecture were sown in the second half of the nineteenth century with the development of iron and glass exhibition halls, train sheds, and conservatories. In the 1880s, William Jenny, Daniel Burnham, and other architects and engineers of the Chicago School developed the freestanding structural skeleton frame that allowed exterior walls to be constructed of lightweight materials, to have large, glazed openings, and to have expressive qualities independent of the building's structure. This method of building, however, was considered suitable only for industrial and commercial buildings well into the twentieth century.[20]

"Modernism" is a term used to describe everything from Bauhaus, the International Style, Art Deco/Streamline Moderne, Mid-century Modern, Brutalism, De-constructivism, and parametric (computer generated) design. What all these subsets have in common is the rejection of visual forms, particularly ornament, found in pre-twentieth-century architecture. Expressions range from rational—where the parts are subjugated to the whole—to romantic—where the whole is subjugated to the parts. Mies van der Rohe summarized the rational approach when he declared "less is more" to which Robert Venturi replied some fifty years later "more is not less."[21] Significant modernist buildings on campuses of the Eight Schools, from mid-century to the present, span the range of these expressions. In the 1950s, Andover hired The Architects Collaborative—headed by Walter Gropius who had come from the Bauhaus to lead Harvard's Graduate

Choate Rosemary Hall
Paul Mellon Arts Center

The Lawrenceville
School
McClellen House

School of Design—to design a group of five dormitories in a natural setting near Rabbit Pond. Gropius had earlier advocated Modernist design for college buildings and "the trustees must have thought that what was good for the colleges would also be good for Phillips Academy."[22] At St. Paul's School in the early 1960s, Edward L. Barnes—an architect based in New York City and known for his museum designs—designed a new grouping of dormitories in his signature minimalist style.

In the early 1970s, Phillips Academy Exeter commissioned Louis Kahn[23] to design the Class of 1945 Library, signaling a departure from

EIGHT SCHOOLS CAMPUS AND CULTURE

the school's revival style legacy. About the same time, Choate Rosemary Hall commissioned I. M. Pei and Partners—a New York City based firm that had designed the East Wing of the National Gallery—to design the Paul Mellon Arts Center, the school's first modern building. These were bold steps that broke the adherence to the revival styles that had defined the campuses of the Eight Schools.

In 1966, Robert Venturi published his "gentle manifesto" *Complexity and Contradiction in Architecture* that reopened the dialogue with architectural history that the modern movement had attempted to stifle. Over the next two decades, some architects incorporated historical references in their work and developed a style that became known as Post-modernism. At the same time the Eight Schools were beginning to accept the rational version of modern architecture, post-modernism was moving toward the romantic version. On campuses with an abundance of romantic architecture, particularly the Colonial Revival and Queen Anne versions, this style fits well. In 1986, for example, Lawrenceville built the Crescent dormitories and in 1996, a new library designed by Graham Gund of Boston. These buildings, while they serve contemporary needs, are compatible stylistically with the nearby Circle dormitories from the 1890s.

In the 1990s and the first decades of the twenty-first-century, a contemporary Modernism, yet to be named, has emerged that is stylistically free and attuned to larger issues of context, scale, community, open space, landscape, and sustainable design. The Eastman Center (music) at Hotchkiss, the Koch Science Center at Deerfield, and the Lanphier Center (mathematics) and Kohler Environmental Center at Choate Rosemary Hall are all exemplary in this regard. (Photographs of these buildings are in Chapter 2.) The proposed field house and the performing arts building at Exeter are the most recent contribution to contemporary modernism at the Eight Schools. This group of projects indicates a trend for choosing prominent architectural firms capable of performing their best work for an Eight Schools' client.

Hotchkiss, however, has shown an ambivalence toward modern architecture. The school's leadership showed great sensitivity in establishing the school's design identity from its founding up to World War II. In 1963, the school ventured into modernist architecture by hiring an alumnus, T. Merrill Prentice, to design the Griswold Science Building. The selected site for the school's first freestanding academic building is northeast of the main building, sandwiched between Gilbert's early infirmary—later re-purposed as a dorm—and the even earlier Bissell Hall dormitory, later demolished. The need to expand the science building in the late 1990s gave the architects, S/L/A/M, the opportunity to envelop the existing building in red brick and add a pitched roof with chimneys, mullioned windows, and white painted trim. This remodeling relates much better to Gilbert's building and a quadrangle of dorms built to replace Bissell Hall, but it obliterates Prentice's modernist design.

When Hotchkiss decided to replace the original main building with a new building in 1970, the school again selected a modern architect, Hugh Stubbins.[24] While the floor plan of the building served the school well, many considered the main, north, entrance and abutting towers un-welcoming. In 1983, Evans Woolen relieved some of the "fortress-like" aspect of the towers with large windows while respecting Stubbins' aesthetic. In 2005, however, the school hired Shope Reno Wharton to infill the inverted V of the south facade with program space and to create a new entrance portico. Both are designed to greet visitors with the by-then traditional

The Hotchkiss School
Main Entry

The Hotchkiss School
Bissell Common

"Hotchkiss Georgian" identity.

    The school hired the architectural firm headed by Robert A. M. Stern to design two additional dormitories (2007) and to replace Bissell Hall (2017). During his tenure as dean of the Yale University School of Architecture, Stern encouraged a wide range of design expressions. His firm's preference, however, was for historically influenced design when the context suggested such an approach. Hotchkiss could not have

The Hotchkiss School
The Bulls

made a better selection. The three dorms form a quadrangle—known as Bissell Common—similar to the ones developed by Gilbert and Delano & Aldrich before the 1930s but without the entrance drive which bisects the earlier quadrangles. Stern's floor plans accommodate contemporary living arrangements but his exterior design is very much in the Georgian Revival tradition.

ART ON CAMPUS

Architecture and the visual arts, particularly sculpture, share a common aesthetic. The grounds of many college and university campuses are populated with sculpture and their art galleries are filled with paintings and other media.[25] The Eight Schools follow their example but on a more modest scale. These art works contribute to academic coursework and the identity of the institution. Upon passing through Scoville Gate to the Hotchkiss central campus, for example, one is surprised to see three reclining bronze bulls on the lawn. Andover features the only purpose-built, free-standing art gallery, The Addison Gallery of American Art. Other schools display their collections and host faculty, student, and traveling exhibitions in galleries within campus buildings. Exhibitions are often related to current courses offerings. Sculpture may be abstract, such as *Seven Generations* at Choate Rosemary Hall, or figurative, such as the life size *Deerfield Boy* and *Deerfield Girl*. Objects may be partly scientific and artistic, such as the *Armillary Sphere* on Andover's Great Lawn and the *Longitudinal Dial* outside the Hess Art Center at Deerfield. Portraits and busts of distinguished heads of school, alumni, and faculty are often displayed in the main school building, library, chapel or other public venues.

Summary

According to the standard set by Vitruvius some 2,000 years ago, buildings are judged by their ability to integrate durability (firmness), convenience (commodity), and beauty (delight). This judgment may be rendered today by various stakeholders including: the stewards of a campus' physical assets; faculty and students who use the spaces provided for their benefit; the campus community, visitors, alumni, and others.

Notes

1 - Vitruvius was a Roman architect during the first century before the Christian Era. His *Ten Books on Architecture* are an encyclopedic account of design theory and construction technology of his time. Vitruvius' criteria of durability, convenience, and beauty appear in Book One, Chapter Three.

2 - The building, assumed to be the work of Charles Bulfinch but later disproved, was not given the Bulfinch name until after the 1936 renovation. Charles Bulfinch had designed the seminary's classroom building, Pearson Hall, in 1817.

3 - *Academy Hill: the Andover campus*, page 20. Brechin Hall Library and the Stone Chapel were the two out-of-place and out-of character former seminar buildings.

4 - Choate Rosemary Hall, page 82.

5 - Style may be viewed as a position on a continuum with Rational on one end and Romantic on the other. Everything in between is a hybrid with an emphasis on one or the other. Rational may include attributes such as order, clarity, ideal, universal, literal, minimal, static, refined, measured, restrained, and others.
Romantic may include attributes such as intuitive, additive, picturesque, pluralistic, dynamic, organic, exuberant, expressive, and others.
Robert Venturi in *Complexity and Contradiction in Architecture* states his preference for "messy vitality over obvious unity." Messy vitality tends toward the Romantic, while obvious unity tends toward the Rational.

6 - Palladio had visited Rome five times to "see and measure everything with my own hands in minute detail." In 1554 he published two guidebooks, one titled *The Antiquities of Rome* and the other *Description of Churches*. The guidebooks are compiled in an English translation by Vaughn Hart and Peter Hicks, published by Yale University Press in 2006.

7 - *American Building*, pages 3–11.

8 - Ashlar masonry is defined by rectangular slabs, horizontally aligned courses, and minimal width joints.

9 - In the early twentieth century the style was adapted by architects such as Ralph Adams Cram and James Gamble Rogers for buildings on college campuses, hence the name Collegiate Gothic.

10 - *Academy Hill: the Andover campus*, page 131.

11 - Henry Hobbson Richardson (active 1860s to 1880s) graduated from Harvard College and attended the École des Beaux-Arts before establishing his office in Boston, and later Brookline, MA. He designed many buildings in his signature style, Richardsonian Romanesque, including Trinity Church in Boston, two academic buildings at Harvard, and several town libraries in Massachusetts.

12 - Cruickshank, Dan, editor. *Sir Bannister Fletcher's A History of Architecture,* page 1146. Other aspects of the "so-called" Queen Anne style include the American shingle style and the English Arts and Crafts.

13 - *The shingle style and the stick style*, page 42.

14 - *Space, Time and Architecture*, page 425.

15 - Dating from the 1930s, the following buildings are among the clearest examples of European Modernism in the U.S.: Chrysler Building and Empire State Building in New York City; Pennsylvania Savings Fund Society building

in Philadelphia, Harvard Biological Laboratories in Cambridge, MA; campus of the Illinois Institute of Architecture in Chicago; and Lovell beach house in southern California.

16 - *Hotchkiss, the Place*, page 20.

17- Collegiate, or Scholastic, Gothic buildings at St. Paul's include Henry Vaughn's Upper School dormitory, James Gamble Rogers' schoolhouse, and Charles Klauder's dormitory quadrangle.

18 - *The shingle style and the stick style*, pages 37–39.

19 - *Theory and Design in the First Machine Age*. European architects formed the International Congress for Modern Architecture (CIAM) in 1928. Members who emigrated to the U.S include Walter Gropius (Germany-Boston), Mies van der Rohe (Germany-Chicago), Marcel Breuer (Hungary-Boston-New York), Eliel Saarinen (Finland-Michigan), R. M. Schindler and Richard Neutra (Austria-Southern California), Jose Luis Sert (Spain-Boston); Alvar Aalto lived in Finland but spent time in Boston as professor at M.I.T. Le Corbusier, one of the most influential European modernists, lived in France and lectured extensively in the U.S.

20 - *American Building*, page 3.

21 - *Complexity and Contradiction in Architecture,* page 23. Venturi's later response to van der Rohe's "less is more" was "less is a bore."

22 - *The Campus Guide: Phillips Academy Andover*, page 114.

23 - Louis I. Kahn (active 1930s–1970s) one of America's most revered architects, practiced architecture in Philadelphia and taught architectural design at Yale University and the University of Pennsylvania. His preferred building material was structural concrete, enhanced by wood finishes. The Salk Institute in La Jolla, CA, the Kimbell Museum of Art in Fort Worth, TX, and the Yale Center for British Art in New Haven, CT, are among his most influential works.

24 - Hugh Stubbins (active 1960s–1990s) designed the first academic and student life buildings at Hampshire College, part of the Five College Consortium, in Amherst, MA. The campus opened in 1970 around the same time Stubbin's Main Building at Hotchkiss opened. His portfolio includes academic buildings at Harvard and Princeton, a presidential library, and several urban high-rise office buildings.

25 - The Princeton University Art Museum, for example, has an encyclopedic collection for teaching and public access, and a collection of outdoor sculpture dispersed across the campus.

Choate Rosemary Hall
Looking Southeast

9: THE WHOLE STUDENT AND THE WHOLE CAMPUS

The sense of being in an architectural space. . . . cannot be understood except by being there[1]
                              Paul Goldberger

There are places I remember, all my life though some have changed, some forever not for better, some have gone and some remain . . . in my life I've loved them all[2]
                              John Lennon and Paul McCartney

THE DESIGN OF A CAMPUS and the culture of a school are synergistic. The previous chapters presented different aspects of the whole student and the whole campus. What is the synergy that results in a coherent whole?

PREP SCHOOL CULTURE

In her paper "What is Culture?" Helen Spencer-Oaty—a Professor of Applied Linguistics at the University of Warwick, UK—quotes a number of anthropologists, 164 to be exact, from the 1860s to the present to discern the nature of culture. One quotation is directly applicable to the title of the book: "It is desirable to distinguish three fundamental levels at which culture manifests itself: (a) observable artifacts; (b) values; and (c) basic underlying assumptions." Regarding artifacts, Spencer-Oaty observes "this category includes everything from the physical layout, the dress code, the manner in which people address each other, the smell and feel of the place, its emotional intensity, and other phenomena…"[3] An indication of values and underlying assumptions of campus artifacts can be found in "moments of truth," that is, pivotal decisions that determine the course a school will take and the one that it forsakes.

Decisions regarding their buildings and grounds made by St. Paul's School, Northfield Mount Hermon, The Lawrenceville School, and Phillips Academy Andover reveal a distinctive cultural value of each school. These choices were precipitated by significant forces that re-shaped the schools: St. Paul's deliberation over the fate of its original chapel at a time of reevaluation of the meaning of a church school; Northfield Mount Hermon's decision to sell one of its campuses and consolidate on the other to achieve coeducation; Lawrenceville's transformation from a proprietary for-profit high school to a boarding school modeled on English precedents; and Andover's tug-of-war over the direction of future development: east or west.

The motto of St. Paul's School is "Let us learn those things on earth, the knowledge of which continues in heaven." It is no surprise

St. Paul's School
Old and New Chapel

Northfield Mount
Hermon School

that the Chapel of St. Peter and St. Paul is the most architecturally significant building on campus. This quasi-cathedral, however, was not the first chapel built by the school. The old (1858) and new (1886) chapels existed side by side until 1952, when a debate arose among trustees and other influential alumni of whether to demolish or retain the old chapel. Advocates of demolition cited the cost of maintenance and infrequent use of the building for religious functions. This discussion occurred at a time when the relevance of a church school itself was being debated, and when the value of preserving historic buildings for their cultural importance had not yet been fully recognized. Proponents of keeping the old chapel cited its historical importance: it was the first building constructed on campus; funds for building were contributed by the founder of the school; memorials to the founder's family were embedded in the windows and furnishings; and spiritual associations with the first rector—who preached served there for thirty-six years—were still evident. Although the trustees initially voted to demolish the old chapel, opposition from faculty and alumni persuaded them to reverse their decision. "That it (the vote) should have been taken in the first place suggests how far the school's history, and perhaps how far its religious values, had declined."4 The return to the founding historical and spiritual values, represented by the "both-and" decision, has guided the school ever since.

For Northfield Mount Hermon School, no such "both-and" outcome was possible. Consolidation of the campuses of the Northfield School for girls and the Mount Hermon School for boys was an educational and financial necessity. Since the schools shared a common history and governance, the mechanism for consolidation was in place. The question of which campus, however, was debated over a three-year period (2000–2004) and only a "Solomon-like choice" could resolve the dilemma.5

Northfield, Massachusetts, is the birthplace, hometown, and gravesite of Dwight L. Moody, the founder of both schools. The Northfield campus is vested with "essential physical elements of the Moody legacy" as well as the architectural quality of the nineteenth-century buildings and the picturesque features of the natural setting.6 There are few buildings on the Mount Hermon campus that compare favorably with Northfield's Auditorium, Russell Sage Chapel, and Marquand Hall. These values were offset, in

The Lawrenceville School
"The Old School"

the judgement of the trustees, by their assessment that the Mount Hermon campus "provided a better setting for building strong community life" and "offered more room to build, including good sites around that central green." The sale of the Northfield campus—which provided capital for the consolidation and preparation for a coeducational school on the Mount Hermon campus—was accomplished, but with much angst.7

The Lawrenceville School faced a challenge to its core values around the time of its centennial celebration in 1910. The "Old School"—Maidenhead Academy, founded in 1810—had evolved over seventy-five years into the Classical and Commercial High School run by Dr. Samuel Hamill. In 1879, the time of the transformative John C. Green gift, the "school was to be the Green Foundation and was to be considered as having no previous existence. It was originally intended to tear down the old school buildings . . ."8 This old school-new school rift continued until the early 1900s, when the then current headmaster and trustees admitted that "this policy was clearly a mistake." The old school alumni were gradually welcomed back by the creation of an alumni association, publication of an alumni magazine, and offers to accept naming gifts, among other enticements. Publication of Owen Johnson's *Lawrenceville Stories*—which evoked the male camaraderie, and shenanigans, of campus life in the old school era—invigorated older and more recent alumni. In planning for the centennial celebration, school leaders further acknowledged the value of uniting the old and new schools. The transformation from a proprietary, for-profit school to "the establishment in perpetuity of a great endowed school"[9] and the assimilation of the old school's alumni attest to the character of the institution.

Phillips Academy Andover's value judgement was precipitated by Andover Theological Seminary's decision in 1908 to sell its land and architecturally significant buildings on the east side of Main Street. In the 1860s, the academy trustees had made a major commitment to develop a campus on the west side, separate from the theological seminary and closer to the town and the Abbott Female Academy. When the seminary property was offered for sale, the academy trustees seized the opportunity. In the midst of active planning and development of the campus on the west side of Main Street, they called time-out. A lengthy and heated debate between "west-siders" and "east-siders" ensued. There were practical arguments for the east side and aesthetic arguments for the west side but, ultimately, the fund-raising power of several wealthy alumni trustees dictated the outcome: the eastsiders won. Their cause was strengthened by the visionary plans and persuasive personality of their allied architect Charles Platt. This combination of vision, money, and persuasion—through personality and power—characterized this critical era in Andover's history.

As discussed in Chapter Seven, the shift to the east side had some negative consequences. The remaining academy buildings on the west side seem orphaned. Today, with the nearly full build-out of the east campus, the strategic importance of the west side land has increased. Platt's Vista allowed for, even encouraged, future development on the west side. The consequence, however, of his disregard for the historical importance of several buildings on the east side—because they were either in the way or stylistically out-of-favor—was an irreversible loss.

EMOTIONAL MEMORY

The synergy between culture and campus is further revealed by expressions of campus as a place of memory and wholeness.

What makes a campus memorable? Of course there is no single or correct answer. Each person—the one-time visitor, the four-year student, the long-term faculty member—will have a different experience, one that is likely to change over time. Imagine an alumnus from the all-boys era returning to campus for a class reunion and encountering female students and alumnae. Following are some theoretical and personal insights that probe the relationship of memory, place, and time.

In the 1980's, Christopher Alexander—a professor of urban planning at UCLA Berkeley—and his colleagues developed a theory of how successful environments develop. They educated graduate students in the theory's "rules of growth," and directed teams in the application of the theory to a real-life redevelopment project in San Francisco. After updating their theory based on lessons learned, they published their findings in *A New Theory of Urban Design*. To achieve wholeness in the environment—city, neighborhood, campus—they determined four fundamental features: (a) the whole grows piecemeal; (b) growth is often unpredictable; (c) the resulting whole is coherent; and (4) the whole is "full of feeling."[10]

Alexander's theory, of course, is not the only proposition or practice of urban design. Town and campus planning in the second half of the nineteenth century embraced a "buildings-in-a-park" strategy. Suburban pre-automobile town plans—Llewellyn, New Jersey, and Chestnut Hill, Philadelphia, for example—distributed single-family houses over rolling topography and along curving streets. The late nineteenth-century campus of Princeton University and the Northfield Seminary for Young Ladies preserved a walkable campus and took advantage of sloping sites.[11] While the resulting whole may be coherent, setting buildings apart from one another in a picturesque landscape represents the antithesis of Alexander's model: buildings organizing and surrounding spaces. Architects and planners of the Beaux-Arts school espoused an axial, hierarchical ordering of buildings and spaces. This type of plan works best when development occurs all at once: for example, Daniel Burnham's plan for the 1893 World's Columbia Exposition in Chicago and McKim, Mead and White's plans for the Morningside Heights campus of Columbia University in 1894 and 1903.

The preceding chapters describe how the Eight Schools' campuses developed over generations and centuries. Their development meets Alexander's first two criteria for a successful environment: the whole grows piecemeal and growth is often unpredictable. The third criteria—the whole is coherent—is more subjective but can be appreciated in a subconscious way. One does not necessarily go in search of coherence, but one knows when experiencing it. Lastly, under what circumstances is the whole "full of feeling?"

Dr. Maria Lamia, a psychologist and author, studies and writes about emotional memory. She cites research that demonstrates the "notion that thoughts can trigger emotions just as the activation of emotion can create cognitions."[12] An emotion triggered by a traumatic event, a vision of beauty, a startling revelation, or another powerful experience can imprint a particular place and time on one's memory. On 9/11 and subsequent anniversaries, for example, one can hardly forget the exact place and time, and the fear, when hearing about the attack on the World Trade Center towers.

Dr. Lamia observes "anything that is connected to your senses may be a cue that can ignite emotional recall." Peter Weis—the current Northfield Mount Hermon archivist—spent his childhood on the Mount Hermon campus, and later graduated in 1978. In his introduction to "A Child's Eye View," a chapter he wrote for *Lift Thine Eyes*, he quotes Clare Cooper Morris: "All of us carry the memory seeds of childhood landscapes—those environments we encountered, smelled, dug in, climbed, and explored when our senses seemed most tantalizingly alive. The smell of a certain flower, the call of a favorite bird, the sight of a familiar staircase or porch or attic window can all trigger the floodgate of memories. We explore the place in our mind's eye, almost feeling the texture of that tree trunk, almost smelling the musty odor of grandmother's basement."[13] Weis recalls: "I read the article cited in *Lift Thine Eyes* when I was in graduate school, as part of a public history course. That class was what truly led me to become an archivist."

The following reminiscences of Eight Schools graduates demonstrate how scent, sound, sight, taste, and touch—experienced in a particular place and time—can both create and trigger lasting memories.

This account demonstrates the power of a semi-private transition space to provide a setting

Deerfield Academy
Ephraim Williams
House

for memorable experiences. "The entrance to the old library, a key hangout spot for day students, had a small round portico with worn marble steps. It had a particular and pleasing smell—mineral, damp, earthy—so thick it seemed to give you nutrients. To this day, when I stumble on that scent, I am instantly back at Lawrenceville."[14]

This reminiscence captures the feeling of contentment that hearth and home conjure for a teenager separated from family. The Ephraim Williams House at Deerfield Academy—built in the late eighteenth-century—was once was the headmaster's house and now functions as the alumni office. "The restored living room, comfortably furnished with early American antiques became my favorite place to study. In the winter a fire was always lit in the large fireplace. I particularly remember the creaking wood floors and the aroma of wood smoke. I sometimes think of that fireplace in the Ephraim Williams house when I'm adjusting the logs in my fireplace at home."[15]

Any account of adolescent campus experiences inevitably involves food. Here's one from a student at Deerfield Academy in the 1980s. "Following a hearty, if bland, dinner students would emerge from the compulsory evening study hall in their dorms in search of food. They often stopped at a station wagon parked dependably in front of the Main School Building. The mobile pizzeria was always fogged with steam, was twenty degrees warmer than the typical frosty Deerfield evening temperature, and emanated the most delicious aroma. Now that I live and work in New Haven—where, everyone knows, the best pizza in America is made—I cannot pass a pizzeria without my mouth watering for that tasty late-night comfort food.[16]

As seen in the two following narratives, large-scale, sometimes ceremonial spaces have the power to create a memorable shared experience.

Phillips Academy
Andover
Art Museum

Deerfield Academy's sesquicentennial celebration featured an outdoor pageant witnessed by an audience estimated at 2,000 to 3,000 students, alumni, trustees, faculty, and distinguished guests. Robert McGlynn, an alumnus, gave this first-hand account. "Those of us who were most closely bound in the occasion are perhaps least of all able to articulate its underlying meaning. . . . For beyond the spectacle of the ceremonies was an experience of the heart in which was the real and memorable meaning of the occasion."[17]

It is a tradition for incoming freshmen at Choate Rosemary Hall to walk from the chapel, where the matriculation ceremony is held, up the hill to the main building Hill House. "One of the most poignant moments of my time at Choate Rosemary hall was the Matriculation ceremony. Surrounded by other nervous fourteen-year old peers, I signed the Register that JFK had signed decades before. When the ceremony ended we walked out of the chapel, stepping onto the lush grass of Hill House circle. We were encompassed by upperclassmen who lined the path clapping and congratulating us. I was mesmerized by the boisterous and enthusiastic welcome of the community as well as the grandeur of the school campus lined with large brick buildings accented with white columns. I know I would be proud to call the school my Alma Mater."[18]

The following reminiscences demonstrate the power of beauty to inspire and recall events, places and times. "It was an early spring afternoon on the Andover campus. Several students were lounging on the lawn in front of the art museum. A girl with blond curls wearing a summer sundress suddenly leapt into the tableau with a balletic grand-jeté. She remains, for me, an archetypical vision of youth, beauty, and joy."

An alumnus of the Hotchkiss School

THE WHOLE STUDENT AND THE WHOLE CAMPUS

The Hotchkiss School
The Mars Hotel

recollects his first impression of the campus almost fifty years after he enrolled. "The beauty of the school was something I never took for granted. . . . I was always in awe of the place. I looked down over the lake and I just don't think there was a more lovely view ever created on earth. I fell in love with it instantly, and all I wanted was to go there."[19]

Dr. Lamia poses a rhetorical question: "Why do you think there are so many love songs?" Clearly, music can make deep feelings accessible. "I truly came to love church music at Northfield. The experience of being in a large choral group made an impact on me. Once a year the girls of Northfield and the boys of Mount Hermon put on a combined concert of sacred music, performed in the huge concert hall on the Northfield campus. Whenever I see a televised concert of the Mormon Tabernacle Choir I always think of that concert of sacred music I sang back in 1963!"[20]

Nature is often associated with seclusion and healing, as well as fear and foreboding. The two following accounts, the first of time spent in the woods and the latter of proximity to water, elicit strong memories.

"For generations of Hotchkiss students the Woods have provided shelter of one kind or another. Mysterious, inspiring, educational, and restorative." The Woods embody the "School's wild heart" and is where "layers of history peel away."[21] Over the years, students built several plain one-room cabins in the Woods. The cabin named Mars Hotel was the special project of a student who subsequently died. A plaque near the entrance reads, in part, "Touch these logs. Thank Charlie for its presence and its memories. October 29, 1989."

"Psychologists write that we humans need water in many forms for our lives. I walked and meditated and admired the seasons as the Lower School pond and the Library Pond became the Turkey River. Sixty percent of my body is water; a big percentage of my inner soul continues to be quenched by my warm memories and feelings for the waters of St. Paul's School."[22]

I hope that reading this book has been as pleasurable for you as writing it was for me.

EIGHT SCHOOLS CAMPUS AND CULTURE

St. Paul's School
Library Pond

Notes

1 - *Why Architecture Matters*, page vxi.

2 - In My Life lyrics; Apple Records 1965.

3 - Spencer-Oatey, H. (2012) *What is Culture?* A compilation of quotations. GlobalPAD Core Concepts. http://www.warwick.ac.uk/globalpadintercultural accessed January 15, 2018.

4 - *A Brief History of St. Paul's School 1856–996*, page 114.

5 - *Lift Thine Eyes*, page ix.

6 - ibid.

7 - *Lift Thine Eyes*, page 186.

8 - *History of the Lawrenceville School: 1810–1935*, page 89.

9 - ibid. page 90.

10 - *A New Theory of Urban Design,* Oxford University Press 1987, page 14; quoted by Witold Rybczinski in *"The Campus as Petting Zoo,"* page 90; http://www.architectmagazine.com/design/the-campus-as-petting-zoo accessed January 27, 2017.

11 - *Princeton America's Campus*, page 93.

12 - "Emotional Memories: when people and events remain with you." https://www.psychologytoday.com/blog/intense-emotions-and-strong-feelings/201711/being-triggered-how-emotional-memories-affect-us; accessed February 23, 2018

13 - "Remembrance of Landscape Past," *Landscape 22, Summer 1978,* pages 34–43.
Ms. Cooper is Professor Emerita of Architecture and Landscape Architecture & Environmental Planning at UC Berkeley. She is principal of Healing Landscapes, a consulting firm, and author of, among other books, *Iona Dreaming: The Healing Power of Place–A Memoir.*

14 - Anonymous, Class of 1987.

15 - Anonymous, Class of 2001.

16 - George Knight, Class of 1985.

17 - "The 150th Anniversary Exercises" *Deerfield Alumni Journal, 1949* quoted in *Deerfield 1797–1997: a pictorial history of the academy*, pages 122–23

18 - Jenny Seibyl, Class of 2011.

19 - *Hotchkiss: a chronicle of an American School*, page 552. Jonathan Bush, Class of 1949.

20 - Bobbe Bailey Otis.

21 - Divya Symmers "Back to the Woods: A New Generation Discovers the Wild Heart of Hotchkiss." *Hotchkiss Magazine, Winter 2010,* pages 4–19.

22 - Peter Otis, St. Paul's School, Class of 1965.

APPENDIX
CAMPUS MAPS
COMPARATIVE DATA

BIBLIOGRAPHY

ACKNOWLEDGMENTS

ILLUSTRATION CREDITS

CHOATE ROSEMARY HALL
WALLINGFORD, CONNECTICUT

1 Christian Street and North Elm Street

2 Hill House Circle
　　student center, dining, dormitory,
　　library, chapel (lower left corner)
　　language lab (upper right corner)

3 Memorial Circle
　　humanities center, dormitories

4 Northeast Quadrant
　　science labs, classrooms, arts center,
　　dormitories; future auditorium

5 Upper campus
　　(former Rosemary Hall interim campus)
　　administration, dining, gym

6 Southeast Quadrant
　　athletic center,
　　dormitories (center left)

7 Kohler Environmental Center

EIGHT SCHOOLS CAMPUS AND CULTURE

DEERFIELD ACADEMY

DEERFIELD, MASSACHUSETTS

1 Deerfield River

2 Historic Deerfield Old Main Street

3 Town Common

4 Memorial Hall Museum
(first academy building)

5 Main School Building

6 Dormitory quadrangle
dining hall (left)

7 Dormitory quadrangle

8 Library (center) arts (right) science (left)

9 Athletic complex

10 Lower level playing fields

THE HOTCHKISS SCHOOL
LAKEVILLE, CONNECTICUT

1 Routes 112 and 41

2 Lake Wononscopomuc

3 Beeslick Woods

4 Golf course - 5th hole

5 Town Hill Cemetery

6 Main Building
    academic, student life,
    administration

7 Dormitory quadrangle 1920s–30s

8 Dormitory quadrangle 2000s–10s

9 Science Center

10 Athletic Center

11 Woodchip Central Heating Facility

THE LAWRENCEVILLE SCHOOL

LAWRENCEVILLE, NEW JERSEY

1 Main Street (Route 206)

2 Original school buildings

3 The Circle
    Circle Houses (upper right)
    Chapel (lower right)
    Memorial Hall (lower center)
    Upper (lower left)

4 The Bowl
    Father's (Pop) Hall (upper center)
    performing arts (lower left)

    visual arts (upper left)
    music (far upper left)

5 The Crescent
    Crescent Houses

6 Flagpole Green (construction site)
    library (upper right)
    dining (right)
    science (lower center)

7 Field House

CAMPUS MAPS

NORTHFIELD MOUNT HERMON
GILL, MASSACHUSETTS

1 Connecticut River
    boathouse and dock

2 Lamplighter Way
    main entrance from I-10

3 Grass Hill
    top (north) to bottom (south):
    dormitories, student center, cottages
    dining, chapel, cottages

4 Academic buildings
    science labs, library, classrooms, arts
    (clockwise)

5 Athletic Buildings
    gym, hockey rink, track

6 Farm buildings and fields

7 Athletic fields

PHILLIPS ACADEMY ANDOVER
ANDOVER, MASSACHUSETTS

1 Main Street

2 Old main campus

3 Great Quad
    Samuel Phillips Hall
    former Seminary buildings (3)

4 Great Lawn
    art gallery and library
    chapel and memorial tower
    elm arch

5 Flagstaff Quadrangle
    commons, dormitories

6 Science Center

7 Athletic Center

8 West Quadrangle dormitories

9 The Vista

10 Abbot Circle

PHILLIPS EXETER ACADEMY
EXETER, NEW HAMPSHIRE

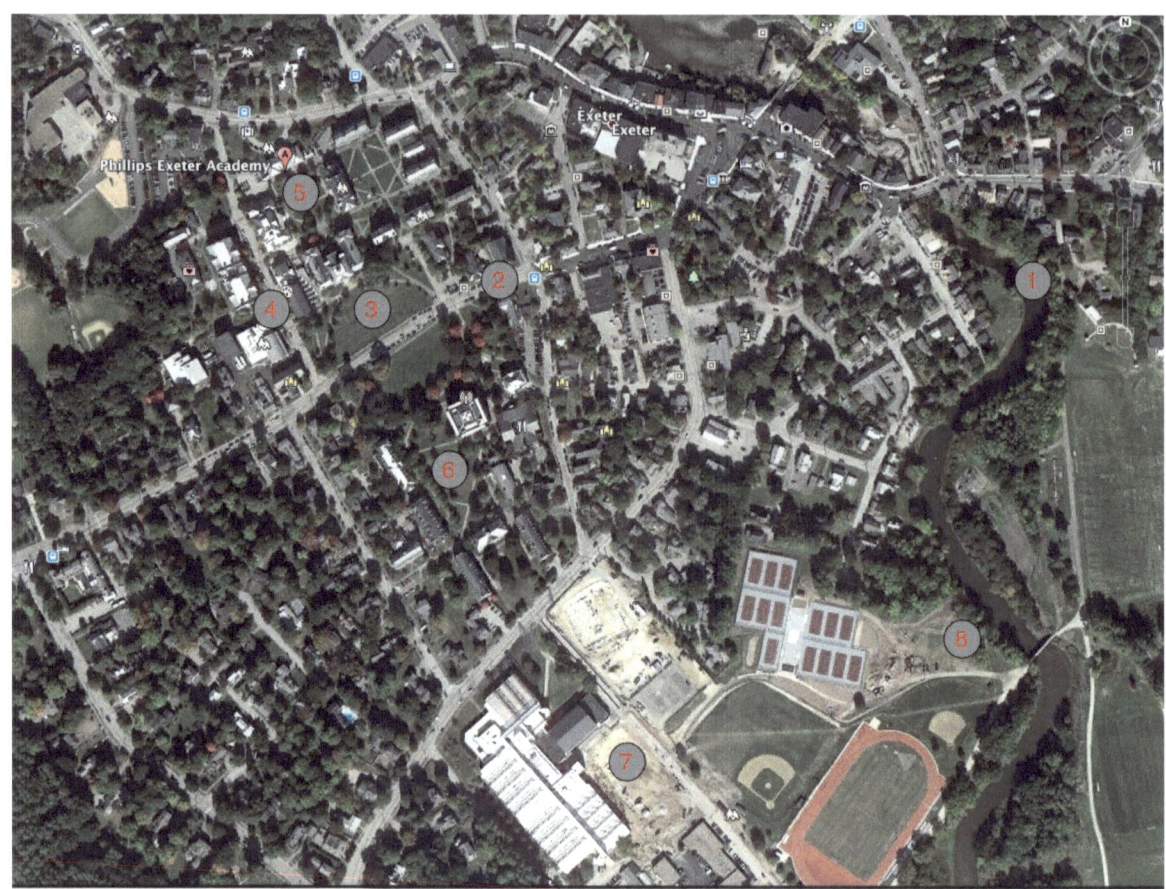

1 Exeter River

2 Front Street

3 Front lawn and environs
   Academy Building, nineteenth-century dormitories

4 Tan Lane
   Phillips Church, music building, art center, science center

5 East and West Quads
   academy center
   administration, classrooms, dining, dormitories

6 South Quad
   library, dining, dormitories

7 Athletic complex
   gyms and fields

8 "Sunday campus"

EIGHT SCHOOLS CAMPUS AND CULTURE

ST. PAUL'S SCHOOL
CONCORD, NEW HAMPSHIRE

1 Dunbarton Road

2 Rectory Road (chapels, rectory, dormitories

3 Dormitories

4 Lower School Pond
  library, hockey center

5 Library Pond
  admission, art center

6 The Meadow and Turkey River
  dormitory quadrangle, performing arts center, central heating plant

7 Academic quadrangle
  science labs, classrooms, auditorium

8 Athletic and Fitness Center

CAMPUS MAPS

COMPARATIVE DATA

CHOATE ROSEMARY HALL
www.choate.edu

Location	Wallingford, CT
Date Founded	1896
Founder	William G. Choate
First head	Mark Pitman
First girls admitted[1]	1971
Total students	859
Boarding	75%
Faculty	118
campus acres	458
endowment	$371 million

THE HOTCHKISS SCHOOL
www.hotchkiss.org

Location	Lakeville, CT
Date Founded	1891
Founder	Mary Bissell Hotchkiss
First head	Rev. Edward G. Coy
First girls admitted	1974
First woman head	not applicable
Total students	598
Boarding	92%
Faculty	155
campus acres	810
endowment	$447 million

DEERFIELD ACADEMY
www.deerfield.edu

Location	Deerfield, MA
Date Founded	1797
Founder	Corporation
First head	Enos Bronson
First girls admitted[2]	1797
First woman head	Margarita O'Byrne Curtis 2006
Total students	648
Boarding	88%
Faculty	125
campus acres	330
endowment	$532 million

THE LAWRENCEVILLE SCHOOL
www.lawrenceville.org

Location	Lawrenceville, NJ
Date Founded[3]	1810
Founder and first head	Rev. Issac V. Brown
First girls admitted	1987
First woman head	Elizabeth A. Duffy 2003
Total students	818
Boarding	69%
Faculty	104
campus acres	700
endowment	$372 million

NORTHFIELD MOUNT HERMON
www.nmhschool.org
Location   Gill, MA
Date Founded   1881[4]
Founder   Rev. Dwight L. Moody
First head   Mary Hammond
First girls admitted[4] 1971
First woman head (of NMH)
                        Jane Robinson 1976
Total students   650
Boarding   82%
Faculty   102
campus acres   1,353
endowment $139 million

PHILLIPS EXETER ACADEMY
www.exeter.edu
Location   Exeter, NH
Date founded   1781
Founder   John Phillips
First head   William Woodbridge
First girls admitted   1971
First woman head
        Kendra Stearns O'Donnell 1987
Total students   1085
Boarding   80%
Faculty   217
campus acres   619
endowment $1,150 million

PHILLIPS ACADEMY ANDOVER
www.andover.edu
Location   Andover, MA
Date Founded   1778
Founder   Samuel Phillips, Jr.
First head   Eliphalet Pearson
First girls admitted[5] 1973
First woman head
        Barbara Landis Chase 1994

Total students   1,150
Boarding   73%
Faculty   218
campus acres   500
endowment $970 million

ST. PAUL'S SCHOOL
www.sps.edu
Location   Concord, NH
Date Founded   1856
Founder   Dr. George Shattuck
First head   Rev. Henry A. Coit
First girls admitted   1971
First woman head   not applicable

Total students   531
Boarding   100%
Faculty   101
campus acres   2,000
endowment $602 million

COMPARATIVE DATA

GIRLS SCHOOLS BEFORE MERGERS

Abbot Academy
(Abbot Female Seminary)
Location	Andover, MA
Date Founded	1828
Founder	Samuel Farrar[6]
First head	Nancy Hasseltine 1854

Merged with Phillips Academy Andover, 1973

Northfield School
(Northfield Seminary for Young ladies)
Location	Northfield, MA
Date Founded	1879
Founder	Rev. Dwight L. Moody
First head	Harriet Tuttle

Merged with Mount Hermon, 1971

Rosemary Hall
Location	Wallingford, CT
Date founded	1890
Moved to Greenwich, CT	1900
Moved to Wallingford, CT	1971
Founder	Mary Atwater Choate
First head	Caroline Ruutz-Rees

Merged with Choate, 1978

Notes

General

Historical data is from school websites and boardingschoolreview.com accessed February 20, 2018.

Heads of school are referred to as headmaster, schoolmaster, headmistress, principal, preceptor, preceptress, rector, or head.

Core campus acreage is usually less than total campus acreage.

Boy/girl ratio varies from year to year; usually about 50:50.

Specific

1 - Choate merged with Rosemary Hall in 1978.

2 - Deerfield was all boys from 1948 to 1989. (see Chapter One)

3 - Lawrenceville was "re-founded" in 1883. (see Chapter Three)

4 - Mount Hermon merged with Northfield Seminary in 1971.

5 - Andover merged with Abbott Academy in 1973.

6 - Samuel Farrar carried out Samuel Phillip Jr., wish to found a girl's school. Farrar was on the board of both the boys school and the girls seminary.

BIBLIOGRAPHY

Alexander, Christopher…[et al.] *A New Theory of Urban Design.* Oxford University Press, New York. 1987

Ambrose, Stephen E. and Sam Abell. *Lewis & Clark Voyage and Discovery.* National Geographic Society. 1998

Banham, Reynar *Theory and Design in the First Machine Age.* MIT Press. 1960

Beattie, Joan M. *Kent One Hundred Years.* The Kent School. 2007

Dober, Richard P. *Campus Planning.* Society for College and University Planning, Ann Arbor, Michigan. 1996

Condit, Carl W. *American Building: materials and techniques from the first colonial settlements to the present.* The University of Chicago Press, Chicago and London. 1968

Cremin, Lawrence A. *American Education: the Colonial experience (1607 – 1783).* Harper & Row, New York. 1970

Cruickshank, Dan, editor. *Sir Bannister Fletcher's A History of Architecture.* Architectural Press Oxford. Twentieth edition, 1996

Echols, Edward C. *The Phillips Exeter Academy: a pictorial history.* The Phillips Academy Press. Exeter, NH. 1970

Evergreen Education Group Keeping Pace with K-12 digital learning. Twelfth edition, 2015

Generous, Tom. *Choate Rosemary Hall: a history of the school.* Choate Rosemary Hall, Wallingford, CT. 1997

Gideon, Sigfried. *Space, Time and Architecture: the growth of a new tradition.* Harvard University Press, Cambridge, MA. Fifth edition, 1967 (original edition 1941)

Goldberger, Paul. *Why architecture matters.* Yale University Press, New Haven and London. 2009

Hamilton, Sally Atwood, editor. *Lift Thine Eyes: the landscape, the buildings, the heritage of Northfield Mount Hermon School.* Northfield Mount Hermon Publisher, Mount Hermon, MA. 2010

Hanmer, Trudy J. *Wrought with steadfast will: a history of Emma Willard School.* The Troy Book Makers, Troy, NY. 2012

Haskell, Julia and Dyer, Davis. *After the Harkness gift: a history of Phillips Exeter Academy since 1930.* University of New England Press, Lebanon, NH. 2008

Heckscher, August. *St. Paul's: the life of a New England school.* Charles Scribner's Sons, New York, NY. 1980

Heckscher, August. *A Brief History of St. Paul's School 1856-1996.* The Board of Trustees of St. Paul's School, Concord, NH. 1996

Herbst, Jurgen. *Once and future school: Three hundred and fifty years of American secondary education.* Routledge, New York, NY. 1996

Jordan, Phil. *The Lawrenceville School: a bicentennial portrait.* Stone Creek Publications, Milford, NJ. 2009

Kilpatrick, Willian Heard. *The Dutch Schools of New Netherland and New York.* United States Bureau of Education, Bulletin 1912, No.12. Government Printing Office. 1912

Kolowrat, Ernest. *Hotchkiss: a chronicle of an American School.* The Hotchkiss School. 1992

Matthews, Laurie. *A Circle in Time: Frederick Law Olmsted's Design for The Lawrenceville School.* Master of Landscape Architecture thesis, University of Oregon. 2001

Meacham, Scott. T*he Campus Guide Dartmouth College.* Princeton Architectural Press. New York. 2008

McAlester, Virginia and Lee. *A field guide to American houses.* Alfred A. Knopf, New York. 1984

McLachlan, James. *American boarding schools: a historical study.* Charles Scribner's Sons, New York. 1970

McPhee, John. T*he Headmaster: Frank L. Boyden of Deerfield.* Farrar, Straus and Giroux. New York. 1966

Mondale, Sarah; Patton, Susan B.... [et al.] *School: the story of American public education*. Beacon Press, Boston, MA. 2001

Montgomery, Susan J. and Roger G. Reed. T*he Campus Guide: Phillips Academy Andover*. Princeton Architectural Press, NY. 2000

Moorhead, Andrea and Robert *Deerfield 1797-1997: a pictorial history of the academy*. The Deerfield Academy Press, Deerfield, MA. 1997

Morgan, Keith N., Elizabeth Hope Cushing, Roger G. Reed. Community By Design: *The Olmsted firm and the development of Brookline, Massachusetts*. University of Massachusetts Press, Amherst and Boston, in association with the Library of Landscape History, Amherst. 2013

Mulford, Roland J. *History of The Lawrenceville School 1810 - 1935*. Princeton University Press, Princeton, NJ. 1935

National Park Service, U.S. Department of the Interior. *National Register of Historic Places–Nomination Form The Lawrenceville School*.

Oates, William A. *Views from the Rector's Porch: lessons of a headmaster*. Posterity Press, Chevy Chase, MD. 2013

Rudolph, Frederick. *The American college & university: a history*. The University of Georgia Press, Athens GA. Reprint 2009 (original edition A. Knopf, New York 1962)

Stern, Robert A. M. *The Architecture of St. Paul's School and the Design of Ohrstrom Library*. St. Paul's School Alumni Horae. Spring and Autumn 1992

Schmidt, George P. *Princeton and Rutgers: the two colonial colleges in New Jersey* D. Van Nostrand Company, Inc. Princeton, New Jersey. 1964

Scully Jr., Vincent J. *The shingle style and the stick style: architectural theory and design from Richardson to the origins of Wright*. Yale University Press. New Haven and London. 1955 revised edition 1971

Spencer-Oatey, H. *What is Culture? A compilation of quotations*. GlobalPAD Core Concepts. 2012

Sutcliffe, Anthony. *London: an architectural history*. Yale University Press. New Haven and London. 2006

Talbott, Page. *Benjamin Franklin: in search of a better world*. Yale University Press. New Haven and London. 2005

Tignor, Robert… [et al.] *Worlds together, worlds apart*. W.W. Norton & Company, New York, Third edition, 2011

Turner, Paul V. …[et al.] *Academy Hill: the Andover campus, 1778 to the present*. Addison Gallery of American Art, Andover, Massachusetts. 2000

Urban, Wayne J. and Wagoner, Jennings L. *American education, a history*. Rutledge, New York, NY. Fourth edition, 2009 (original edition McGraw-Hill 1996)

Venturi, Robert. *Complexity and Contradiction in Architecture*. The Museum of Modern Art, New York, NY. 1966

Vitruvius. *The Ten Books on Architecture*. Translated by Morris Hickey Morgan, Harvard University Press, Cambridge, MA. 1914

Walker, Barbara, M. *Hotchkiss, the Place*. The Hotchkiss School. 2003, revised 2011.

Wilder, Laura Ingalls and Pamela Smith Hill, editor. *Pioneer girl: the annotated autobiography*/Laura Ingalls Wilder. South Dakota Historical Society Press, Pierre, SD. 2014

Fiction

Johnson, Owen. *The Lawrenceville Stories*. McAlister Editions. Print-on-demand 2015

Knowles, John. *A Separate Peace*. The Macmillan Company, Toronto, Ontario. 1959

Sittenfeld, Curtis. *Prep: a novel*. Random House, New York. 2005

ACKNOWLEDGMENTS

I WOULD LIKE TO THANK Robert Moorhead, painter and designer, for his graphic design skills and enthusiastic support. Robert and his wife, Andrea, are long-time faculty members at Deerfield Academy. Together they wrote *Deerfield 1797-1997: a pictorial history of the academy.* Suzanne LaCroix, who teaches writing at Southern Connecticut State University, copy edited my final drafts. As this is a self-published book and I am no publisher, I relied on Patricia Fidler at Yale University Press and Jan Hartman at Princeton Architectural Press for their expertise.

Although we have never communicated directly, I consider John McPhee a collaborator. Reading his book *Draft No. 4: on the writing process* is tantamount to auditing his sophomore seminar in creative non-fiction at Princeton University. In another of his books, *The Headmaster,* McPhee recounts his student days at Deerfield Academy and his relationship with Frank Boyden.

*****

Archivists at the eight schools graciously gave me access to the schools' archives, providing finding aids, making reproductions, and responding to my follow-up inquiries. Judy Donald at Choate Rosemary Hall walked me through the exhibition she curated for the school's 125th anniversary. She was the first to make me aware of the Eight Schools Association.

Jacqueline Haun at the Lawrenceville School provided many helpful resources and contacts, one being a former student, Laurie Matthews. Without Haun's help, I likely would never have found Matthews' unpublished thesis—for her Master of Landscape Architecture at the University of Oregon—on Frederick Law Olmsted's design of the campus.

I visited Phillips Academy Andover, St. Paul's School, and Phillips Exeter Academy on a trip through Massachusetts and New Hampshire in April 2015. At Andover, the archivist Paige Roberts guided me through the archives, and John Porter, Director of Communication, led me around the campus.

David Levesque, archivist at St. Paul's School, introduced me to the 2006 Sesquicentennial Exhibition, which is now online, and provided reproductions of the 1898 and 1923 reports on campus development by Olmsted Brothers. Paul LaChance, the Assistant Director for Facilities Engineering, gave me an extensive tour of the interior of the Chapel of St. Peter and St. Paul.

At Exeter, long-serving archivist Edouard Desrochers, his successor Peter Nelson, and Nelson's assistant Thomas Wharton provided, among other resources, an out-of-print pamphlet A Walking Tour of Phillips Exeter Academy with the Bicentennial Map, dated 1981. It was a pleasure for me to spend time in the celebrated Class of 1945 Library where the archives are housed.

Driving north on I-91 along the Connecticut River leads to the campuses of Northfield Mount Hermon and Deerfield Academy. Archivist Peter Weis spent his childhood on the Mount Hermon campus and returned some twenty years later. He gave me a tour of the then vacant Northfield campus and provided a first-person account of the consolidation of the two campuses.

Deerfield archivist Anne Lozier provided many documents and insights into the history of the academy. She also introduced me to the two local historical societies: Historic Deerfield and The Pocumtuck Valley Memorial Association.

At The Hotchkiss School, Rosemary Davis, archivist and Joan Baldwin, Curator of Special Collections, helped me unravel the historical tapestry that is the Main building, and to trace the campus planning process through archival reports, drawings, and photographs.

*****

I would also like to thank my friends and colleagues who agreed to read chapters as they progressed and to contribute their diverse perspectives on education, daily life at boarding school, campus planning, and architectural design.

I wrote the first draft of the preface before I started organizing and writing chapters. The preface was, and still is to some extent, reflections of my student days at Kent School. I asked Peter Neely, a Kent classmate, for his feedback. Peter advised me to set it aside and come back to it after I had written the chapters. It was good advice.

Joseph D'Amico—a classmate of mine at the University of Pennsylvania—established a firm to provide educational research and assessment for secondary schools. He read Chapter One (The whole student: education of youth in America). He alerted me to the value and effect of synergy in educational settings.

The aforementioned Peter Neely, an English teacher and administrator at The Thayer Academy, read

Chapter Two (The whole student: teaching and learning). Peter's long career in the independent secondary school environment, as well as his appreciation of campus planning and architecture, were invaluable. His understanding of Christopher Alexander's work was helpful in forming my thoughts for Chapter Nine.

Bill Baskin, a graduate of The Holderness School and Yale Law School provided preliminary editing of Chapter Three (The whole student: boarding and bonding). As the chapter developed, George Knight, Deerfield Academy Class of 1985 and the Yale School of Architecture, provided many first-person insights into boarding school culture and was an early and enthusiastic supporter of the book. Knight is principal of his architectural firm in New Haven and teaches at the Yale School of Architecture.

Jenny Seibyl, a graduate of Choate Rosemary Hall, class of 2001, read Chapter Four (The whole student: diversity and inclusion). Her perspective as a female day student was a refreshing change from the male boarding student found in most printed resources. She kept me on track in transitioning between Choate and Rosemary Hall when they were separate schools, and during the lengthy implementation of coeducation.

Peter Otis, a 1965 graduate of St. Paul's School, read Chapter Five (The whole student: body and soul). He played hockey and rowed crew at St. Paul's and served in the Acolytes Guild, Chapel Advisory Committee, and the Missionary Society. He is semi-retired from his position as Director of Career Services at the Yale School of Forestry and Environmental Studies.

Shavaun Towers, former principal in the landscape architecture firm Towers | Golde, read Chapter Six (The whole campus: natural setting and town). Her firm consulted on the site portion of master plans and/or implementation projects at nearly twenty independent schools—including The Hotchkiss School, Choate Rosemary Hall, and St. Paul's School—and thirty colleges and universities. She helped me understand the concept of a pedagogical landscape.

Patrick Pinnell, an architect, town planner, and author read Chapter Seven (The whole campus: physical and financial planning). His firm's portfolio includes, among other projects, private houses, historic preservation, iconography, and new town planning. He wrote the first and second editions of *The Campus Guide: Yale University*.

Aaron Helfand graduated from Deerfield Academy in 2001 and—after college and graduate school—earned a MPhil in the History of Architecture from the University of Cambridge. His reading of Chapter Eight (The whole campus: art and architecture) clarified several stylistic distinctions. Helfand practices architecture in New Haven and is a board member for the New England Chapter of the Institute of Classical Architecture & Art.

Patricia Fidler, publisher of art and architecture at Yale University Press, read Chapter Nine (The whole student and the whole campus). She helped me focus my narrative and restructure some of my sentences. With her eagle eye, she proofread the final draft.

Aaron Helfand (author), George Knight (illustrator), and I (photographer) are currently working on The Campus Guide: Deerfield Academy, scheduled for publication by the Princeton Architectural Press in February 2020.

*****

Finally, I want to thank my wife, Patricia, our daughter Clare, and our dog Pawson for their love, intelligence, and good humor. My daughter Lydia Barnett, assistant professor of History at Northwestern University, has supported and critiqued my various writing projects.

ILLUSTRATION CREDITS

Unless noted below, all photographs are by Robert Spencer Barnett

Preface
The lovely valley land of Kent; courtesy of Kent School
The merry pranksters; Kent 1963 yearbook
Author 1962; Kay Prindle

Chapter One: Education of Youth in America

Noah Webster; Root & Tinker, 1886; Library of Congress,
Portrait of Catharine Beecher,
    possibly by W & F Langenheim; courtesy of Harvard University, Schlesinger Library on the History of Women in America, Radcliffe Institute
American Progress, John Gast, 1872; George A. Crofutt 1873; Library of Congress
Keystone Academy Beijing, rendering; web download
Deerfield High School and Deerfield Academy, Allen Sisters, 1878 Courtesy of Pocumtuck Valley Memorial Association Memorial Hall Museum, Deerfield, Massachusetts

Chapter Two: The whole student: teaching and learning

Third Academy Building courtesy of Phillips Exeter Academy archives
Harkness classroom c.1967; courtesy of Phillips Exeter Academy archives
Big Study library c.1873; courtesy of St. Paul's School archives
Lanphier Center i.d.lab; courtesy of Choate Rosemary Hall

Chapter Three: The whole student: boarding and bonding

Shattuck summer home c.1858; courtesy of St. Paul's School archives
Churchill House c.1880; courtesy of Phillips Academy Andover archives

Chapter Four: The whole student: diversity and inclusion

Rosemary Hall campus plan 1925; courtesy of Choate Rosemary Hall archives

Chapter Five: The whole student: body and soul

The big gym c.1903; courtesy of Choate Rosemary Hall archives
The old gym c.1885; Walter R. Merryman; courtesy of Phillips Exeter Academy archives
Hockey Rinks c.1884; courtesy of St. Paul's School archives
Rowing course 1958; courtesy of St. Paul's School archives
Rowing course; courtesy of St. Paul's School archives
Chapel enlargement c.1928; courtesy of St. Paul's School archives

Chapter Six: The whole campus: natural setting and town

View from Mount Holyoke, Northampton, Massachusetts, after a thunderstorm–The Oxbow, 1836.
    Thomas Cole; Library of Congress
Aerial view of campus looking northwest; courtesy St. Paul's School archives
Aerial view of Northfield campus looking east 1913; Lithograph by Littig & Co., courtesy of North field Mount Hermon archives
Aerial view of Mount Hermon campus looking west 1913; Lithograph by 1.Littig & Co.; courtesy of North field Mount Hermon archives
Aerial view of consolidated campus looking south; courtesy of Northfield Mount Hermon
Master Plan 1992; Prentice & Chan, Ohlhausen; courtesy of The Lawrenceville School

Chapter Seven: The whole campus: physical and financial planning

A view of the buildings at Yale College at New Haven. Published April 6th, 1807 by A. Doolittle & Son. Yale University buildings and grounds photographs, 1706-2004 (inclusive). Manuscripts and Archives, Yale University
Seminary Row c.1830; courtesy of Phillips Academy Andover archives

Model of The Idealized Andover, 1928. Photograph by
    H.F. Chance; courtesy of Phillips Academy
    Andover archives
The Vista, 1932. Rendering by Charles A. Platt;
    courtesy Phillips Academy Andover archives
Abbot Academy The Circle; courtesy of Phillips Academy
    Andover archives
Aerial view of campus looking northwest c.1905; courtesy
    of The Hotchkiss School Archives and Special
    Collections
Gilbert General Plan Dated 1915 and 1925; courtesy of
    The Hotchkiss School Archives and
    Special Collections
Aerial view of campus looking northwest c.1970; courtesy
    of The Hotchkiss School Archives and
    Special Collections
Main Plan 2001; courtesy of The Hotchkiss School
    Archives and Special Collections
Campus plan 1972; courtesy of Phillips Exeter Academy
    archives

Chapter Eight : The whole campus: Art and Architecture

Wells-Thorn House; Aaron Helfand
Russell Sage Chapel c.1938; courtesy of Northfield Mount
    Hermon archives
Memorial Hall; courtesy of The Lawrenceville School
    archive

Chapter Nine : The Whole Student and the Whole Campus

Aerial view of central green; courtesy of Northfield Mount
    Hermon

Appendix

Campus aerial backgrounds; Google Earth

ROBERT SPENCER BARNETT, AIA, received his Master of Architecture degree from the Columbia University Graduate School of Architecture, Planning, and Preservation. He taught construction technology courses at the Southern California Institute of Architecture and the New Jersey School of Architecture at NJIT, and served as project manager and Vice President of Gruen Associates in Los Angeles and Director of Design Technology at the Hillier Group in Princeton.

Most recently, Barnett served Princeton University in several capacities, including Vice Provost for University Space Planning, Assistant Director of the Office of Physical Planning, and Program Manager in the Office of Design and Construction.

His large-format black and white photographs of cast iron buildings in lower Manhattan were exhibited at the New York Historical Society (group) and the MIT Rotch Library (solo).

His book *Princeton University and Neighboring Institutions,* a title in the Campus Guide Series, was published in 2015. *Hindsight–Foresight: from the founding to the future of five Ivy League campuses* was published in 2012.

THE AUTHOR

DESIGN BY A&R DESIGN

TEXT SET IN ADOBE GARAMOND PRO

ILLUSTRATION CAPTIONS SET IN ADOBE JENSON PRO

PRINTED IN THE UNITED STATES OF AMERICA

www.ingramcontent.com/pod-product-compliance
Lightning Source LLC
Chambersburg PA
CBHW041547220426

43665CB00003B/56